"If everyone who gambled in America followed the guidelines in my book, the casinos would close down."

LYLE STUART'S NINE COMMANDMENTS OF GAMBLING

- Never gamble when you are tired or unhappy.
- Never forget that the longer you stay at any casino table, the larger are the odds that you will walk away a loser.
- Never begin to play unless you know at exactly what loss-point and/or win-point you will quit.

For the other six commandments and a wealth of winning advice, please begin reading

CASINO GAMBLING
FOR THE WINNER

CASINO GAMBLING
for the
WINNER

Lyle Stuart

BALLANTINE BOOKS • NEW YORK

Library of Congress Catalog Card Number: 77-28279

ISBN 0-345-28338-4

This edition published by arrangement with Lyle Stuart Inc.

Manufactured in the United States of America

First Ballantine Books Edition: October 1979

Back jacket photo by Harry Benson

Contents

Introduction

This is a book about casino gambling written for the man or woman who is determined to win.

It isn't for those who visit casinos for fun or to play games or to ". . . only lose x-dollars" or to "make my donation."

I have flown on jam-packed junket planes where more than two hundred junketeers were being ferried back from Las Vegas to New York after a three-night/four-day "free" visit to a top hotel-casino. I could not locate a single winner in the entire lot.

Keep in mind that most of the people on the plane were there because they were known "high rollers"—larger-than-usual bettors. Therefore, risking larger than usual sums of money, they should know more than the average player about winning.

Winning is not the name of their game.

If you are one of the many millions who visit Las Vegas for a good time, some good shows, some tennis or golf, some good food and drink and perhaps some extracurricular sex, this book *isn't* for you.

Rather, this book is for that rare person who has some notion of what gambling is all about and who wants to know if there is any way at all to beat the casinos.

There is.

For many years I have been most skeptical of people who were going to share their secrets about how to make millions in the stock market, win at the races, etc. If they knew, why would they share their valuable knowledge for a few additional dollars?

My feelings were confirmed when, after twenty-one years of casino gaming, I found that I was able to win on 10 consecutive visits to Los Vegas. (More about the 11th visit later.)

"You ought to write a book," my friends would say.

"Why?" I asked. "Why in the world should I share what I've learned when I paid so much dues to learn what I know?"

The answer did come. Friends wanted to know all about it. From Mario Puzo to Bob LeShufy and from David Geller to a nameless acquaintance who considers it a victory if the hotel maid will give him half a dozen towels for a $3 tip—(which towels he happily packs into his suitcase!)—they all seemed fascinated as I returned with reports of win after win.

The answer came because friends who are obsessive (as distinguished from compulsive) gamblers listened carefully to my new-found wisdom—and then went their merry ways doing their same old things and losing the same old ways.

I realized, finally, that many thousands might read this book but only a few dozen would apply its wisdom in action. The casinos can afford those winners, and I can afford that much competition!

At any rate, you are about to read what may be the most savvy book you have ever read about casino gambling. And probably the most valuable.

Although I'm neither shy nor modest, my first instinct was to make this an impersonal account. So impersonal that originally I thought I'd use a pseudonym.

But then I changed my mind. If this was to be "the most authentic approach to winning" it had to be the most honest.

I am therefore sharing it *all* with you. The winning trips and the losing ones, too. It will be a first-person chronicle all the way.

That being the case, I will herewith disclose the record of the first ten visits I made to Las Vegas in 1977. The amounts of money listed are net profit over all expenses including first class air fare (usually provided by the casinos), all food, drink, hotel accommodation, car rentals, tips, bets for the dealers (substantial), and even the charges for parking my car at Kennedy Airport in New York.

Visit #	Date	Hotel stayed at	Amount won
1	Jan. 1–3	Caesars Palace	$ 18,600
2	Jan. 8	None	$ 10,700
3	Jan. 20–23	Riviera	$ 9,400
4	Feb. 6	None	$ 14,265
5	Feb. 23–27	Riviera	$ 7,412
6	March 16–19	Caesars Palace	$ 36,009
7	March 28–29	The Aladdin	$ 29,990
8	April 7	Riviera	$ 3,457
9	May 12–15	Caesars Palace	$ 22,093
10	May 27	None	$ 14,579
Total winnings for 10 trips to Las Vegas:			$166,505

How did I do it?

Patience, dear reader. You've got to creep before you crawl. So let's start at the beginning. . . .

LYLE STUART

1

Background

There will be narrative and there will be anecdotes in this book but there will be no wasted words and no padding. That being the case, I'm going to assume that you know the basic rules of the casino games. If you don't, buy a two-dollar book somewhere and learn them. This is a university class: not a kindergarten.

If you know casino gaming, you'll know that the following observation is unnecessary for you. Scan it anyway. Let's end the age of innocence immediately by understanding this statement:

CASINO GAMES WERE NOT DESIGNED TO FAVOR THE PLAYER.

It's worth repeating, so read it again. And keep it in mind. Those people on the other side of the tables didn't build those eighty million dollar palaces as gestures of charity. The rules of the game were created to give you pleasure and to give the casino your money.

"Doubt that the stars are fire, and doubt that the sun doth move," as Prince Hamlet said to Ophelia . . . but do not doubt what you have just read.

Every game in the casino has a one and only objective, the separation of you from your money. Some games will take it more rapidly than others. They all have the advantage of odds against you, or what I shall refer to as the percentages.

Let's illustrate it with the machine: the slot machine. Let's say that the machine is fixed to pay out 90% of what it takes in. You may insert a dollar and get back $25 or $2,500. But of all the dollars inserted, the payoffs will not exceed 90%. If you put in $10 you'll get $9 back. If you reinsert the $9, you'll get $8.10 back. If you insert $8.10, you'll get back $7.29. And so forth until you've given it all to the machine.

Now, obviously, dollar machines don't return dimes, nickels and pennies. Obviously, too, wins and losses are random so that you might put in $10 and win $100 or lose all $10. But the machine is pegged to pay back 90¢ for every dollar inserted and will, in time, take its full toll from the players.

Robert Mazzocco, writing in *The New York Review*, describes the one-armed bandits as "stacked back to back like markers in a graveyard."

No sophisticated gambler will ever be seen playing slot machines—not even those advertised as "The Hottest Slots In Town." They are for mindless players . . . for wives of gamblers who have time to pass . . . for people who are largely too dull or too lazy to learn the rules of the other games in the casino.

Despite the high purchase price and accompanying high license fees and taxes on slot machines, they are particularly profitable because there is so little human labor involved in running them. Low-paid change girls, a mechanic for repairs and a supervisor make them ripe profit plums for every casino.

At the end of 1975, there were 48,757 slot machines

licensed in Nevada. These produced such rich profits for the two hundred casinos in Nevada that 32.8 percent of the state's total taxable gambling revenue came from slot machines.

Slots, however, are not your worst bet in the casino. Keno can take a 25% slice of your investment. That's why they have so many comfortable chairs with armrests in the Keno hall. Keno is the game that pays for the chandeliers and those neon signs on the street.

Does anybody win big at Keno? Does anyone really win $25,000 for an investment of a dollar or two? Sure. When Milton Prell opened the Aladdin, one player won $10,000 four times within twenty-four hours. Improbable, you say? Yes, but true. We're going to deal with the improbable later in this book.

The managers of the Aladdin were disturbed but not distressed. They knew that in time they would win all that money back. . . .

The next worst major game in a casino is roulette. As long as the casino has both the "0" and "00" and plays American instead of European casino rules, the odds of 5 and 5/19 percent are much too heavily stacked against you.

If you favor roulette, save your air fare and send the casino a check for your probable loss. Sure, there are occasional winners. There are occasional winners in the Irish Sweepstakes, too. But the rules of the game are such as to make this one of the casino sucker games. Avoid it.

I once had an incredibly lucky experience at the casino in Monte Carlo when I thought I had lost the equivalent of $100 on a bet, walked across the casino to the cashier's cage to buy more French francs, and when I returned learned that my 2 to 1 bet had won, had won again and had won again. I thought I had been playing the bottom 12 numbers and instead I'd accidentally bet on the top 12. I picked up chips worth $2,700 for a profit of $2,600.

It was luck, plain dumb luck. But it failed to endear me to roulette, even European style.

Charles DeVille Wells inspired the song, "The Man Who Broke the Bank at Monte Carlo" by winning £50,000 in two days and nights at the tables. He wound up serving eight years in prison for fraud and died broke in Paris in 1926.

That leaves three games serious enough to mention. If you are a mathematical genius, and a person with a sharp eye and a marvelous memory, you'll incline toward blackjack. In which case this book isn't for you. Trade it for a copy of *Playing Blackjack As a Business* by Lawrence Revere.

To win consistently at blackjack, you have to become a card counter. As of this writing there's a case in the Nevada courts to force casinos to let card counters play. As of now when the casino spots you as a card counter, they will make your life unpleasant by asking you to leave in any one of a variety of ways. They want you out of the casino.

I have personally known many card counters from Mannie Kimmel to Revere himself. I haven't known one who has won *consistently*. Counting may invert percentages, but it doesn't do away with the element of luck. Even the best counters win a few and lose one. I know one counter who thought he had them fooled. He worked up a stake of more than $40,000 in winnings in three visits. And then one night his wife refused to join him for dinner, and he went to the tables angry and disgruntled. In a short time he lost $80,000. He's still paying off against his markers.

There are enough books, systems and courses available about blackjack. I play it only rarely. If I'm running "lucky," I'll make a maximum bet—or five of them at one time—and then manage my money so that if I'm lucky on the first go 'round, I must quit winners.

If you're looking for blackjack advice and tips here, you've climbed the wrong mountain. In these pages we're going to concentrate on two games: craps and baccarat. They offer the best shot a casino will give you. They take the smallest percentage. They require no counting, no cheating, no "smart guy" stuff. They are the only games worthy of your hard-earned dollars.

But first to some basics and how I came to know them.

The Internal Revenue Service doesn't worry about getting its fair share of player winnings. Its gaming experts know that the big tax income will come from the casino side. They understand house percentages better than most players.

2

The beginning of knowledge

Twenty-one years ago I flew to Las Vegas for the first time. I flew in a propeller-driven plane that took eight hours to get there. I really didn't go to gamble. I was on my way with my family to Beverly Hills and remembered that my friend Paul Denis had said that I must see Las Vegas because "it's the way the world is going to end."

That intrigued me.

The year was 1956. Joe E. Lewis was playing at El Rancho Vegas (later to burn down in a fire of mysterious origin) in a show which featured the incredibly beautiful Candy Barr. Most of the major hotels of today didn't exist. There was a place called Sans Souci ("without care") which is now the Castaways. The New York mob had opened a very fancy hotel, The Tropicana. It was designed for the bluebloods. The people with the fancy names, furs and fortunes all came to the opening: the Astors and the Vanderbilts and the Whitneys. They chatted with each other and stared at each other.

The surroundings were lush. The food was superb. Everybody was happy except the Tropicana's owners. It turned out that bluebloods are not, as a class, heavy gamblers.

Others made similar mistakes. A plush watering hole was built on the strip for millionaires who didn't want to gamble. It was called Tally-ho. It had no casino. It was built with something that tried hard for English Tudor style but with no deep forethought about its purpose. Why, for example, would a non-gambling millionaire want to visit Las Vegas?

After two groups of owners dropped large amounts of money, Milton Prell bought Tally-ho and converted it to the Aladdin.

But back to my first visit in 1956.

I elected to stay at The Tropicana.

I knew nothing about casino rules. I didn't understand dice. Blackjack looked simple enough, but it would be years before a computer expert said, "Split aces and eights and always draw to 17 if the card the dealer shows is 7, 8, 9, 10 or ace. If the dealer shows 2, 3, 4, 5, or 6—draw only until you have 12 or better."*

For starters, I tried blackjack.†

---

*The rest of this simple strategy, of course, is always split 8's and double down on 10 and 11 if the dealer shows 6 or less; always split aces; split nines against a 4-deck shoe (but not against a 1 or 2 deck hand dealer), and always draw to a soft 17—namely an ace and a 6. Play blackjack only for relaxation and only for small units of money. Not only doesn't the player realize how heavy a percentage is going for the house; even the house doesn't know how much is going for it! Treat the blackjack table the way you would a pinball game. Nickels—but no big dough.

†Technically the casino game is "21"—for in the true game of blackjack, the first person dealt a total of 21 in two cards becomes the new dealer or banker. In "21" the casino always deals.

Each hand called for thought and a decision. Of course it was a "no way" situation, and I lost $1,500.

My wife and two children sunned themselves poolside next to Eddie Fisher and Debbie Reynolds and their children. The food was good. In those days a midnight buffet with literally half a hundred separate food choices and all you could eat was available for $1.50. Liquor was free. Rooms were modestly priced, and in our room there were flowers.

The $1,500 I dropped was about half the cash reserve I had in the world. I thought about it and decided that rather than concern myself with this loss, I would concentrate on raising my income. I did. Considerably.

That was the year I launched a book publishing company with a single title, and established a company now worth many millions of dollars.

I began to learn the rules of the games. It has always fascinated me that a person will spend years getting an education in order to acquire a skill that will pay off in good income and then will go to a gambling casino and waste much of that good income on games in which the person has almost zero knowledge.

I acquired some knowledge. As the years went by and the level of my bets increased, I became a "high roller" and was given the special courtesies that high rollers receive and deserve.

I was comped wherever I chose to stay. "Comped" means that air fare, room, food, liquor, shows, etc., are compliments of the house. The theory is that if you stay at *their* hotel you are more than likely to pay for it all at the tables. Even those who wander from casino to casino are found to do about sixty percent of their playing at the place in which they sleep.

At times my losses were very high. So were my wins. I have lost as much as $30,000 in ten minutes and won as much as $60,000 in twenty minutes.

Luck is a lady but—as with all ladies of class—

chooses her lovers imperiously. Let me cite a single complete experience.

Milton Prell got his start in gambling many years ago when he bought a near-bankrupt bingo parlor in Gardena, California. He examined the operation. Shills were being handed the winning bingo cards in advance.

"Fire the shills," he said; "from now on we're really going to give the prizes to the players."

This was heresy!

"You can't do that," his executives protested. "We'll be broke and closed in five weeks."

"We'll be broke and closed in six weeks the way we're going now," Prell said.

Prell's place quickly won the reputation for being the only honest bingo parlor in town. It thrived. Eventually he came to Las Vegas. With some financial assistance from his brother-in-law, Gil Gilbert, he started the Sahara and the Mint—and built fine reputations for both casinos while he owned them.

When Milton Prell bought the Tally-ho to convert it to the Aladdin, I bought one percent (one point) for $25,000. The hotel needed a bankroll, and Prell had a reputation for honesty. The story went that although most joints kept three sets of books (one for the stockholders, one for the IRS, and the real one) Prell kept only two.

Owning a point seemed like a fun investment and a good one. I could gesture to the thousands of light bulbs outside the hotel and say with pride, "I own one out of every hundred of those!"

To qualify, I had to fill out voluminous forms listing my every asset and its origins. There were forms for the state of Nevada and separate forms for Clark County.

After I submitted the papers, the casino gave me "sky's the limit" credit. (Which is part of the story to follow.)

At this time I was about to publish a book about Howard Hughes. Attempts had been made to stop, or at least to delay, its publication. At a meeting at a town-house on New York's East Side rented from Faye Emerson, attorney Greg Bautzer, representing Hughes, spoke in terms of a hundred or two hundred thousand dollars. I explained that I wasn't about to be bought off or frightened off. He then discussed a deal whereby if I'd delay the book for two years (or until the TWA suit was ended) Hughes would give me or my author a face-to-face interview. It soon became apparent to me that Bautzer was playing a stalling game and I said: No, thanks.

The Hughes machine went into action. An attorney named Chester Davis set up a corporation called Rose-mont Industries which claimed to own all rights in the life story of Howard Hughes. A secret deal was then made with a writer named Ezra Goodman. Goodman's contract with me provided that I wouldn't change a comma of his script. His deal with Rosemont Industries allowed them to edit completely before he submitted the script to me.

For this he received a check from Rosemont Indus-tries for more than $40,000.

I have friends. One of them tipped me off to the deal, and I was able to smoke it out. I sued Goodman in arbi-tration and was awarded the return of the $10,000 ad-vance I'd paid him. He then declared personal bank-ruptcy for upwards of $300,000. I was the only creditor who fought the issue.

Ex-FBI agent Norman Ollestad acted as my Califor-nia attorney. In an unprecedented decision, the bank-ruptcy application was denied. But before I could col-lect my $10,000, Ezra Goodman vanished.

It was in the midst of this scenario that I had to make a personal appearance before the Gaming Board in Carson City. Prell explained to me that there was a lot of static about my license, and it seemed to be coming from the Hughes camp.

My Nevada attorney and I flew from Las Vegas to

Reno. In the morning before our scheduled drive to Carson City, I dropped in to Harrah's, in Reno.

A young man stood alone at the dice table shooting. He put a silver dollar on the line and picked up the dice. I decided to bet with him. He threw a long numbers-packed hand. When he finally sevened out, I had won $8,000; he had lost his dollar.

I tossed him a $100 chip and enjoyed his startled surprise and delight almost as much as my win. Then I joined my attorney for the charade that was to take place in Carson City.

It became apparent after a few minutes of strained double-talk that, as the old expression goes, "the fix was in."

The buy-off was so obvious that some members of the board appeared to be acting out a Three Stooges script. It seems, they explained, that they were objecting to two books in a catalog of 350 that had been distributed by a subsidiary company of mine a couple of years before.

Under questioning, the board members conceded that they hadn't actually seen the books and didn't know their contents but from the couple of lines describing them, decided they must be "obscene."

I pointed out that in my then fifteen years in publishing I had never had the slightest trouble with the law on any level regarding the things I published.

The room was small and occupied by only a handful of observers. These included a cluster of attorneys for Howard Hughes who sat in the back row grinning.

My attorney struggled to cope with the convoluted reasoning that it might be dangerous to grant a license to me. Even if the two titles weren't "dirty" (their word!) I *might* publish something objectionable in the future!

Although my FBI file is reported to be one of the largest in the Bureau's history (turn over in your grave, Al Capone!), in my entire adult life no law enforce-

ment agency has ever accused me of anything more serious than parking in a no-parking zone. Nobody was
accusing the board members of anything either, but one
of the three commissioners felt it necessary to explain
that *he* hadn't been influenced by the Hughes people.

I was turned down. I felt a mixture of amusement
and anger—mostly anger. (We'll address ourselves later
to the business of playing while you're upset.) Five
minutes later, without hearings of any kind, the joker
commissioners granted Howard Hughes a license to
own and operate the Desert Inn.* It was his first Las
Vegas casino. He hadn't filled out the forms and hadn't
bothered to make a personal appearance.

I drove to Lake Tahoe and lost the $8,000 I'd won in
the morning and a couple of thousand more. Then I
drove to Reno and flew back to Las Vegas.

I was staying at The Sands, and when I walked into
the casino I was approached by Charles Turner, one of
the owners. He congratulated me on my "good fortune"
in being turned down because "that joint can't make it."

Both Las Vegas newspapers front page headlined the
turndown. The *Sun*'s Hank Greenspun published the
first of two front page editorials condemning the board

---

*Chester Davis, sober, and Bill Gay, the Mormon Machiavelli,
did quite a job on the Hughes estate. The original Desert Inn
had 500 rooms, cost $2 million to built and paid off its entire
investment within the first year.

After Hughes bought it and conveniently died, Davis and
Gay took control. In 1977 the Desert Inn underwent extensive
"building improvement." Cost? About $70 million. The im-
provement? One extra room for the customers and a 3-story
suite for Bill Gay.

Gay, who doesn't know frog shit from pea soup about
gambling or running a hotel, has a sizable appetite for personal
comfort.

The *Las Vegas Sun* observed that "There is not a contractor
in town who couldn't perform the same work, including Gay's
suite, for less than $20 million and show an exorbitant profit
in the undertaking."

because it would scare off other "responsible business-men."

He called the action "irresponsible" and concluded the first column with the following:

Few of us, no matter what state we live in, are par-agons of virtue and we recognize that Nevadans must be even more virtuous than residents of states where gambling is not legal. But our image can suffer if the rest of the nation laughs at us, too.

The next day, also on the front page, Greenspun re-minded the board of errors the gaming control agency had made in the past. He cited the fact that it had turned down applications from generals in the U.S. Armed Forces.

Greenspun added, "Frankly, sex shocks me once in a great while. . . . And I have been shocked by actions of past control members who carried on shamefully with broads on the Strip. But that doesn't mean I would deny them the right to a livelihood because I don't ad-mire their taste in women or possibly caught them in a compromising situation."

None of this consoled me. I was still angry. I went to the Aladdin. Within a short time at the dice table I had signed $18,000 worth of markers.

Then I seated myself at the baccarat table. There were three shills ("starters") and one real player. He faced me from the other end of the table.

The limit was $2,000, and I was betting the limit. Soon I was $10,000 on the rim. That made $28,000 I owed the Aladdin. Prell's brother-in-law, casino man-ager Gil Gilbert, stood watching the game.

"Gil," I said, "give me another $12,000. That'll make an even forty. If you give me any more, I won't pay it."

If you give me any more, I won't pay it. Those are

the magic words—especially effective where a casino is eager to "stretch and break you."

Within the next ten minutes, I lost another $10,000.

On a couple of occasions the player at the opposite end of the table beat me by such close scores as 5 to 4 and 6 to 5. He was playing $20 a hand. I was playing $2,000.

"Great," I remarked after one such close defeat.

"I don't feel so good winning my small bet when I see how much you're losing," he said. (A kind remark, considering that most gamblers are rightfully "I'm-for-me-first" players.)

I was down to my last $2,000 as the shoe was passed to the other player.

Instead of betting the usual $2,000—I decided to prolong the ordeal. It was around 10 P.M. Once this two grand went, I'd have lots of time to kill. I'd cut off further credit, and I had no wish to see a show, have sex or walk in the desert. Instead of $2,000, I put $300 in the Player box.

"Why don't you go with me just once?" the other player called to me from across the table.

"Why? Are you going to do good?"

"I'm going to make four passes!"

I had consistently bet against him. What the hell, I thought. What's another ten minutes? I pulled the $300 back and pushed all my money onto the Bank side.

He made one pass. A second. A third. Then he dealt a tie.

"Nothing personal!" I said as I followed a belly hunch and pulled the money over to Player. Player won.

Within a few minutes, he and I were laughing it up— calling to each other: "What are you gonna do now?" and playing on the same side.

When he saw what was happening, Gil Gilbert got upset. He leaned over to whisper something in the man's ear. In an instant I was up and racing to the other side of the table.

"What's the matter?" I demanded.

"Nothing, Lyle. I just thought this gentleman was bothering you," Gil said as he lamely retreated.

"Bothering me?" I replied. "Next to my wife and kids this nice man is the best friend I have in the world! Don't bother *him*!"

When the shoe had been dealt out, I decided to cash in.

"Gil, I have an $18,000 marker in the dice pit. Would you get it for me?"

I counted my cash. I had won back all my losses and was now $5,600 ahead. One remark from a stranger had changed my play and resulted in a turnaround of more than $80,000 in less than fifteen minutes.*

---

*When I'd finished counting my money (they played with cash rather than chips in those days) and looked up to thank him, he had vanished. We met again in the same casino a couple of months later. "What happened to you? You disappeared on me! I couldn't even buy you dinner or a drink!"

"Aw," he said graciously, "I could see you were busy so I didn't want to hang around to bother you."

3

That fickle finger

Anyone who has gambled in casinos over an extended period of time can boast of some very happy experiences. And, of course, some memorably miserable ones.

There was a time when I was a regular visitor and winner at The Pair of Shoes casino in London. Dapper Eric Steiner, who liked to call his elegant Edwardian, plush-lined gilt and crystal emporium "a small social club," fronted the place. It was an "in" place for celebrities. On this night, Henry and Clare Luce were in the dining room. Geraldine and Sydney Chaplin were upstairs in the intimate casino. David Susskind sat on a couch surrounded by four beautiful young ladies.

Eric Steiner decided to show off.

"You're a sport," he said to me, as he greeted me. "I'll bet you $1,000 on one roll of the dice."

I agreed. But I didn't agree to go with the player then shooting, or with Bill Cosby, the next shooter. Steiner wouldn't agree that I shoot, and I wouldn't agree to let him shoot. We finally decided on my British cousin, who was in a casino for the first time in her life.

She threw the dice. A 2 and a 1.

I handed Steiner a thousand-dollar bill.

(My cousin later explained that she thought the object of the game was to get the dice as close to the other end of the table as possible!)

I walked over to a blackjack table. Within minutes I had won the thousand back and then some.

Eric Steiner was upset. "Lyle, from now on use this place as your private club. Be our guest for dinner and drinks. But do your playing elsewhere. You're too lucky for us."

It took me a moment to realize he was in dead earnest. I was flattered.

The Pair of Shoes closed some time later amid sinister rumors about the identity of its real owners.

The next night was our last in London. My wife and I visited the Playboy Club.

The dice table had a fifty-pound limit, and I played it and spread out place bets and quickly lost a couple of thousand dollars. The casino was thick with people and thicker with the cigarette smoke that both my wife and I detested. (The place was originally built to be executive headquarters for an appliance distributor, and its ventilation system was designed to ventilate for thirty people rather than three hundred on its narrow floor.)

Mary Louise, who rarely complained, suggested that we go elsewhere. And I, who was rarely cross with her, said with some irritation, "Look, I want to gamble here a while longer. Do me a favor and play some blackjack for a little while."

I felt guilty as she turned and walked away. Then I plunged back into the game. I was about to have a most unusual experience.

I won and I lost, as the dice moved around the crowded table. The trend wasn't decisive. And then it was my turn again, and I was about to have one of those mystical experiences that are every dice player's dream. I threw number after number after number. I made pass after pass after pass. The chips piled up in front of me—for I had all the numbers covered by come bets and topped with odds money.

Dice anywhere out of the U.S.A. is a relatively slow game. There are longer than necessary delays in dice action because dealers are not really skilled in quick and proper payoffs.

So it was that in the middle of the great shoot I was having, a stranger tapped me on the arm and said, "Did you hear about the guy at Caesars Palace who held the dice for half an hour?"

I had indeed heard. But that wasn't the point. As every dice player knows, there are certain firm superstitions about the game of craps:

If a die jumps off the table, the next roll inevitably will be a 7-out. If a die hits somebody's hand, the dice will 7-out. If a wife says to her husband, "How are you doing?" his next roll will 7-out.

It's all garbage but, like many religions, it has a large following.

I was surprised that the man's conversation didn't bother me. I continued to roll and roll and roll. Meanwhile, I kept trying to sight my wife through the smoky room. I felt vindicated by my decision to stay on.

Now I began to show off. I tossed the dice backwards under my arm. Over my shoulder. I bounced them. I tossed them high in the air. I could do no wrong.

Finally I became concerned. I wanted to find Mary Louise to share the news of my good fortune with her.

"I pass," I announced, after making another point.

There was a loud chorus of "No!" and "Don't!" and "Please, don't!"

I picked up the cubes again, and continued to shoot. Finally, as I was coming out for a new point, I announced: "I know how I'll get out of here! My odds are working!"

(It's a house rule that the odds placed on come bets don't work on the come out roll unless the player says otherwise. Thus, if the shooter throws a 7, the odds money is returned to him while the casino keeps the come bets.)

I threw a 7.

Slowly the dealers picked up the bets from fifteen players. They took my place money and my odds money. The entire jam-packed ring of people at the table had been mesmerized by my hand.

Only when the stick man started to push the dice to the next shooter did somebody come out of the trance to shout, "Wait a minute! He *won*! He rolled a 7!"

Pandemonium broke loose. Assistant managers rushed to assist the dealers in their crisis.

Each player was asked the amount of his wager. It was reconstituted and then paid off. Again and again the dealers would say, "But, sir, you were only betting one pound not ten——" and a supervisor would say with resignation, "Pay him. Put ten pounds on the line and pay him off with another ten. It was our mistake."

The dice were mine again. I continued to throw them for another ten minutes. When finally I sevened out, the gentleman in charge announced: "Ladies and gentlemen, this table will be closed for a short time."

There was a chorus of moans, groans and protests.

Through the smoke-filled room I suddenly spotted Mary Louise at a distant blackjack table. I was in a hurry to share the good news but first carried my bundle of chips to the cashier's cage. The man who seemed to be in charge of things was standing there waiting for me.

"Why did you close the game? Were my dice too lucky?"

"No," he said. "But you've cleaned out the cage. You've broken the bank."

I thought he was jesting. He was quite serious. I was asked to accept all kinds of European currency as well as all kinds of money orders. The cashier was still short $2,600, so a Playboy check for that amount was made to my order.

I returned to New York and deposited the check.

Weeks later, I asked my comptroller why the check hadn't cleared. Our bank told him that the Bank of England was being unusually slow in clearing checks. Two days later, England devalued the pound.

I wrote to the Playboy Club with a copy of my bank clearance slip. I pointed out that I had lost $260 in the devaluation although it wasn't my fault that their cage didn't have funds enough to pay me fully in cash.

The Playboy people were okay about it. Back came an airmail note of apology with a check for $260.

The Playboy experience had been another lucky one. But I was an average "high roller" who won and lost large amounts and knew only slightly more than most "low rollers" what it was all about.

4

I give up gambling

I was tempted to begin this book with a warning against gambling. All gamblers are fools. Any gambling that risks your losing enough money to affect your standard of living or add to your worries is self-destructive. The best gamble is not to gamble at all. I was then going to add that if you accepted that premise and were going to gamble anyway, this book could be helpful.

I don't happen to be a compulsive gambler. Compulsive gambling is a very serious disease. I have watched a man lose his entire business overnight. I have known another who couldn't face his gambling debts and committed suicide. For those with the disease, I strongly recommend a phone call to Gamblers Anonymous.

I may go to the racetrack once a year as a social thing. Gambling at the track bores me.* So does baseball and football betting. I don't gamble on any of the

*I don't like to bet on anything that breathes but can't talk back to me to explain why it didn't do what it was supposed to do!

Islands (people who gamble in Puerto Rico are compulsive losers), and I no longer gamble anywhere in Europe for reasons which will become apparent. Months and months have gone by when I didn't have time for a visit to Vegas and didn't give it a second thought. Nor have I ever lost more money than I could comfortably afford to lose—that is, than I could pay without affecting the living standards of my family.

In 1969 my wife died in my arms in a house in Port Maria, Jamaica, of cancer. She died without taking a painkiller (though local doctors couldn't understand how she endured the pain) because she wanted to be conscious of her family to her dying breath.

For a long time after that, I really didn't give a damn about anything. When I went to Las Vegas, I lost large amounts of money. Shortly before her death I had received one check for $498,000 from the sale of stock and I didn't have anything to do with the money.

The pattern was set. There were times when I won, but more often I lost. My playing was listless and drugged. I didn't give it much thought. One year after her death, I took twenty-four members of my publishing staff on a bonus vacation to Los Angeles, San Francisco and Las Vegas. Four hotels gave me three rooms each, and all of my staff were comped.

While some of my young men from the shipping room were waking up to champagne and breakfast steaks, I had become an unwilling tour director and by the time we all left town, I had in my weariness dropped $140,000.

A few weeks later *Life* magazine was researching a feature article about me and asked that I go back to Las Vegas so I could be photographed in the casinos. I dutifully did. Of the fifteen or so photographs that were published to illustrate the article, only one resulted from that visit. On which occasion I dropped another $60,000—making for a neat $200,000 loss in two months.

I had no feelings about any of it.

Time passed and the listless losing pattern continued. Eventually a girl named Carole Livingston became my frequent companion. One day she and I were guests at Caesars Palace for the Alan King tennis classic (I still don't know where the tennis courts are) which was a celebrity-studded affair.

It seemed that every third face you saw was someone you recognized from the television or movie screens. But the super-star was obviously Sidney Poitier—for while people stared at and pointed to the other celebrities, they grouped around Poitier as though he were the Pied Piper.

I avoided Poitier. He and I had been in the same weekly poker game for many years and occasionally we'd lunched together. He'd known of my wife's illness, and I'd thought he'd have sent her a card or made an encouraging phone call. Nothing.

When the news of her death appeared in *The New York Times*, he twice called the office of mutual friend producer Philip Rose for my home phone number. But he didn't call me, and I hadn't heard from him.

So it was that whenever I saw him in the casino, I detoured to avoid a meeting.

At about 2:30 A.M., Carole and I saw a huge crowd following Sidney and Diana Ross (then currently headlining the show). The two seated themselves at an empty blackjack table. They were surrounded by a couple of hundred gapers.

"Let's move closer," Carole said. "I want to see what he looks like."

"You know what he looks like," I said, irritated. Sidney had, in fact, visited our offices and patiently posed for an individual Polaroid picture with each member of our staff.

We arrived at the back edge of the crowd just as Sidney moved around on his stool, surveying the darkened casino. He wore the glazed look of the celebrity who has been stared at long and hard.

Suddenly he did a double-take and swung around again.

"Lyle!" he called out, jumping up. The crowd parted to allow him through as he came at me. I held out my hand stiffly and said a cold "Hello, Sidney." He pushed my hand aside and embraced me.

In the course of conversation, he asked about my children. (You can't be angry with someone who inquires about your children.)

I asked how he was doing.

"How do you mean?"

"At the tables. Here."

"I don't gamble anymore."

"What do you mean, you don't gamble? What about the poker game?"

"I haven't been in the game for nearly two years."

"Why?"

What followed couldn't have taken more than a minute and a half. I have often wished that I could have taped it. He made the point that when you give money to a casino, you are spitting on your family and on everything that you've achieved in your career. He also made the point that if you had surplus money to disburse, you could better spend it on protein for some of the hungry peoples of the world. But no summary here could do justice to what he said.*

Even as he finished speaking, I realized that he was right.

I joked about why he hadn't talked to me $59,000 sooner. I promised to try to catch up with him when he played tennis at 10 A.M. that morning, but at 10 A.M. that morning Carole and I were in the car—having decided to leave town.

---

*He also told me that to convince himself that he was through, he'd bought $10,000 worth of chips and carried them around in the casino for an entire day without making a bet.

On the way to the airport, I swung left and pulled into the driveway of the Aladdin. The valet took the car, and as we approached the entrance doors I remarked to Carole, "This is an historic moment."

She didn't know what I was talking about.

I had decided to give up gambling for a while. Sidney Poitier's ninety-second sermon had put things into perspective.

I'd stopped off at the Aladdin because up to that time and from the day I had almost become an owner, I had never been a loser at the Aladdin.

Within a few minutes I had won about $5,000, thus reducing my net loss for the visit to $54,000.

On the further drive to the airport, I mentioned to Carole that I believed I wouldn't be gambling again for a while. I wasn't giving it up forever, but what Sidney said made sense to me. He had talked about gambling in a context that I'd never before considered.

For the next two years I didn't make a wager of any kind. Not even to the extent of buying a New York State lottery ticket.*

---

*One of the worst wagers you can make—to be sure—but the year before I'd bought four 50¢ tickets for my daughter, Sandy, and she'd won $5,000 on one of the tickets.

5

Life is just a bowl of cherries

Early on, I shared with you the results of my ten winning visits to Las Vegas. Contrary to what you might think, they weren't pure luck (though, of course, I had been lucky) and they weren't accomplished dishonestly or with any edge except a reasonably rigid adherence to a combination of the wisdoms I am going to impart to you in the pages that follow.

But, first, I want to tell you what my thinking was.

Having decided to give up casino gambling for a while, I would from time to time consider beginning to play again.

One thing I thought about was that during the years of my marriage I had won sometimes and I had lost sometimes. But my Mary Louise, playing for small amounts of money, had come away winners fourteen out of sixteen times.

Fourteen out of sixteen times!

What was *her* secret?

For one thing, she knew the rules of the games she played (blackjack and craps).

She had an interesting philosophy. She believed that in almost every contest with the casino there is some point at which the player is ahead. That's the point at which you quit.

You quit winners!

Moreover, if anything bothered her at a table: the attitude of another player . . . a remark by a dealer . . . the smoke from a cigarette or a cigar—she would get up and walk away. Promptly. Without hesitation. For she believed that one had to be in a happy and affirmative mood if one was to make correct decisions and to properly manage one's money. Any irritation could work to one's detriment.

Those were the seeds that developed into the approach that I am going to set out for you in the pages that follow.

Some of it is going to disturb you. Some of it may clash head-on with your own deeply-held beliefs. It has only one thing going for it: it has worked ten times in a row.

I've known many people who have gambled regularly in Las Vegas. I have never known any of them to win ten times in a row. These people range from Mannie Kimmel (who is "Mister X" in books by Thorpe and John Scarne and who is said to have once lost half a million dollars on a single bet on a presidential election) to Nick the Greek and include casino owners, managers, pit bosses and dealers. Nor have any of them been able to tell me of anyone who has won that consistently.

Think about that. Then pay special heed to the guidance that follows.

Sometimes, to make you get the point, I will repeat myself quite deliberately. And some of what I tell you will be paradoxical and have its own built-in contradictions. But all told, what you are about to read is razor-sharp and guru-true.

6

The first rules of the game

The first and most important thing you must understand if you are to become a steady winner is *The contest is not between you and the casino. It is between you and yourself.*

Winning in a casino is a matter of self-discipline. If you are savvy, you know *what* to do. (Or you can learn.) But unless you are disciplined, you won't do it. And in time you will lose. You must set your own rules—*and follow them*. To the extent that you do this, you will win. To the extent that you don't, you will inevitably fail.

Rule 2: *Hit and run.* The casinos will hate you for it, but IT IS THE ONLY WAY YOU CAN CONSISTENTLY WALK AWAY WITH THEIR MONEY.

In almost every game you play, there will be a time when you are ahead. Put aside a part of that, the money you're ahead and your original stake, so that you MUST

LEAVE THE TABLE A WINNER and if you are to lose, lose only the small portion left.

You can never go wrong walking away with a profit. Never worry about what you "might have won" if you lingered longer!

Failure to follow this strategy is why most people are losers in Las Vegas and everywhere else casinos operate. Incidentally, studies have shown that women are better able to do this than men. With men, there seems to be a self-esteem problem. Ego gets in the way of wisdom and so men play on, losing back what they've won—and then are driven by pride to try to recoup that.

You know the syndrome.

Women are not as ego-involved and are much better able to walk away winners and leave the ego-feeding for the suckers.

The importance of what you have just read can't be stressed too strongly. There is no way you can play any casino game over an extended time and come away winners. Percentage will grind you out. Long losing streaks will destroy all of your plans and systems.

It is for this reason that some casinos won't pay air fare for a player unless the player stays three nights. (If you don't lose your bankroll in three nights, you aren't really trying!)

On some junkets for smaller-money players, the casino requests three or four hours of play a day with $25 chips.

The job of the people who run those abattoir-efficient casinos is to keep you playing until you lose your stake: Your job is to play until you have some of their stake—and then beat a happy retreat.

7

Knowing the score

In Las Vegas there is a splendid book shop known as the Gamblers Book Club.* It issues monthly bulletins and offers the most complete collection of gaming books in the world. Read everything you can on the game or games of your choice. Knowledge is win-power.

There is a newsletter called *Rouge & Noir*. It keeps you informed of changes in rules, limits, etc.†

These are tools of knowledge. They can't hurt and they could help. Having said that, please dwell on this next sentence.

---

*John Luckman, a former dealer, operates it with his wife. It's worth visiting at 630 South 11 Street. Or write for catalogs to Box 4115, Las Vegas, Nevada 89106.
†*Rouge & Noir* is $25 a year and easily worth it. Their address is Box 6, Glen Head, N.Y. 11545.

THERE ARE NO SYSTEMS

There are approaches . . . there are good wagers and bad wagers . . . there are money management tricks. *But there are no systems that will defeat any casino game over any period of time.*

If you don't accept this, you're a cherry-flavored lollipop. The more you're willing to wager on your system, the more readily the casino will send that special plane for you. Or, as the old casino manager's directive goes: "When you find a system player, send a taxicab for him."

If you are looking for a sure-fire system, you are Jason in search of the Golden Fleece. And it's you who are ripe for the fleecing.

There *are* gaming approaches and attitudes. The only "system" is a combination of the rules and attitudes that I offer you in these pages. If you believe otherwise, you're a true believer and a natural victim.

8

The beginnings of winning

Time out to review the first three commandments, and to look at a fourth.

1. Self-discipline
2. Quit when you're ahead
3. There are no systems

Get 'em? Got 'em? Good!

Now let me tell you about Louis Holloway. Holloway is a delightful old fellow who has earned a living gambling and has done it for some thirty-five years. He is the author of the book *Full-Time Gambler*.

Holloway has a son reputed to be a mathematics genius.

"Dad," said the son one day, "you can't win against a casino. You can't beat the odds. You just can't."

"You're absolutely right, son," Holloway replied. "Do you see this house we're sitting in? That automobile outside? Remember that college tuition paid for you each semester? They all came from casino winnings. But you're absolutely right."

Holloway is a professional gambler. I made the rounds with him on a few occasions. I watched him win at blackjack, and I watched him win at dice.

Until a heart condition limited his activity, he played each day for an hour to an hour and a half. He won $40 to $75 every day. Then he quit for the day. He played seven days a week. He spent other hours reading every new piece of literature to come out on every phase of gaming. He analyzed and discarded every system "guaranteed" to win.

Holloway is a counter at blackjack. But nobody pays any attention to him. His bets are $2 and $5. He looks like an innocent minister on a fun binge.

He exemplifies our next rule of the game.

DON'T BE GREEDY.

Greed is a major ally of the casino. It stops you from following the QUIT WHEN YOU'RE A WINNER rule because when you're running good, you don't want their cash alone; you want the chandeliers, too.*

Greed is a natural enemy of self-discipline. It's a disease that causes you to lose perspective. You know that over any long play the casino will win. And yet you sit there or stand there unwilling to walk away with a big score because you want an even bigger one.

Let me recite two examples that I know about firsthand. A busboy at the Frontier went to a casino on Fremont Street where a friend was dealing blackjack. The busboy had exactly $16 in his pocket. He played at his friend's table.

This was no setup. In fact the dealer quickly relayed

---

*Don't mistake the thrust of this advice. Too many casino patrons let losses run up but limit their winnings. A casino shift boss once remarked about someone I know: "He's dangerous because he presses when he wins and if you're not careful, he'll write you a new address!"

to the pit boss that he knew the player and was told it was okay to deal to him.

The busboy got very lucky. He went from blackjack to the dice table. He moved from the Mint to the Golden Nugget and then to Binion's Horseshoe.

By 2 A.M. he had won more than $9,000.

He taxied back to his room near the Strip hotel where he worked. $9,000! He couldn't sleep. An hour later he was back on Fremont Street. By sunrise he had lost it all.

Arnold Bruce Levy runs a mail order book business in New York City. He got very lucky. He won $52,000. He and his girl went up to their room with the big pile of money. She pleaded with him to get a cashier's check or to put some in safekeeping. He told her not to worry. He put it all under the mattress.

If a pea kept a princess from sleeping, try to imagine what $52,000 did to Arnold Levy. He couldn't sleep a wink. He was a very restless fellow.

"Please, don't," his girlfriend pleaded when he got up and began to dress.

"Hell's balls!" he announced. "I'd be crazy to quit when I'm on this great streak! I'm going downstairs and double it!"

When the couple returned to New York's Kennedy Airport the next day his girlfriend had to lay out cab fare to Manhattan.

If you know gamblers, you know the story over and over again.

Here's rule #4 again:

DON'T BE GREEDY.

9

Going with the trend

The information that I'm going to impart in the next few paragraphs can easily be worth one hundred times the cost of this book to anyone who gambles in casinos for more than silver dollars.

Irving Berlin wrote a song for a Fred Astaire film. The song, "Cheek to Cheek," mentions a gambler's lucky streak.

There *are* lucky streaks. There will be times when you can do no wrong.

There are also unlucky streaks. During which time you won't be able to win a bet to save your backside.

I am indebted to Louis Holloway for the following rule. It has saved me a fortune.

Let's use as an example a game we don't play: roulette. Red has come up three times in a row. What do you do?

I'm certain half of my readers would chorus: "Bet black. Black is bound to come up!"

Wrong.

You have one of two choices. You bet red or you don't bet at all.

Why? Because one thing the sophisticated gambler knows is that the improbable *can* happen. Red could come up in the next fifteen times. Or fifty.

Three, for our purposes, is considered a streak.

You must bet with the streak or not at all.

If you bet and you're wrong, you've lost one bet. If you bet against the streak and you're wrong, you can keep betting and you can be wiped out.

This approach has a dual purpose. It allows you to get in on streaks, and it prevents you from becoming emotionally involved in bucking a trend.

If three passes are made at the crap table, you bet with the shooter or not at all. If three shooters in a row miss (fail to make a pass), you bet on the "Don't pass" side or you don't bet at all.

At the baccarat table, if three hands in a row are player (or bank), you bet with that side or not at all.

I have just saved you a lot of losing moments and cut down your chances of being sucked into a losing quicksand.

Gamblers have an advantage over non-gamblers. Quite apart from the thrills and the chills, one learns many life-lessons at the gaming tables. Gambling like life is fraught with uncertainty. Uncertainty is what it's all about.

One of those lessons is that in a casino, as in life, the improbable can happen and often does.

I am one of the world's worst poker players. Let me cite a lesson that I learned at poker.

One night in a game of 7-card stud, a new player to the game had two queens showing. I had a full house with kings, and the betting got hot and heavy. Ours was a table-stakes pot-limit game.

He showed four queens.

The next hand, shuffled and dealt by a new dealer using the alternate deck, gave me a neatly concealed

full house—this time with aces! Again as the raising
and reraising heated up, the other players dropped and
I was facing the same opponent who had just beaten me
for a lot of money. I saw my chance to recoup as he bet
into me. I raised back. Carefully. Enough to incite him
to reraise. Then I had him count his chips and tapped
him out. I had tried to figure his hand. He showed three
pictures which suggested either a straight or a flush. He
called.

"One thing I know you don't have," I had blithely
remarked, "is four queens."

He had four queens.

The odds against a player having four queens twice
in a row are astronomical. Literally millions to one. But
that means that once in those millions of hands, someone somewhere will, indeed, have four queens twice in a
row.

Respect the probability of the improbable.

The scene was the baccarat table at the Aladdin.
Each time as the shoe went around, I would build up
my stake. Each time I had the shoe, I bet $4,000 on
Bank. Four times the Player hand was "natural nine."

It was my fifth shot at the shoe. I put down my last
$4,000. "I don't care if I lose this bet," I announced to
one and all, "but I'm gonna be very annoyed if I lose it
to another natural nine."

My hand was eight. Worthless against the player's
eight and ace—another natural nine.

Five hands and each defeated by nine. $20,000
worth of experience in relearning that the improbable is
always possible.

10

Getting rich without trying

I heard this story first-hand, but I didn't see it happen so I offer it without sworn affidavits.

He's an elderly fellow and a very high roller. And this is the story he told me:

"I'd had a losing session at the blackjack tables, and I was walking to the cage to cash in a few small chips. Something was happening at a dice table that attracted my attention, because there was a larger-than-usual crowd of spectators. A young man was the shooter. Before he rolled, he kissed the dice; his girl kissed the dice and then he kissed his girl. It was a funny routine, and he did it with every toss of the cubes.

"Suddenly I latched on to the fact that he'd been doing it for a couple of minutes. The crowd loved every minute of it. I had $130 in my hand in chips. I placed the 6 and 8 for $60 each and pocketed the remaining two $5 chips.

"For a while the young man threw almost nothing but sixes and eights. I spread profits to the other numbers. He threw the other numbers. By the time he sevened out, I required five racks for my black chips ($50,000) and I handed $200 to the casino porter who helped pick up some of my chips that fell to the ground. The shooter had won a big $127, and I gave him $500."

The man who told me the story is not a braggart. He is a high-stakes player. As an experienced gambler, he had the instinct to get in on a hot roll.

Again and again you will find that most players freeze as an improbably lucky streak takes place in front of their eyes. The experienced gambler has the instinct to jump in—even if it's in the middle. Even, in fact, if the next roll is the end of the streak.

The story is an old familiar one. It has happened from the first roll of the dice and the first turn of the playing cards.

Take this report from a subscriber to the now-defunct newsletter *The High Roller*. It appeared in 1968. The reader reported:

> One night in February of this year at about 11 P.M., I wormed my way into a very crowded crap table in Caesars Palace with a stake of $500. The table was full of high rollers. Things got very cold and player after player left the table—but I was determined to stay until I had a roll of the dice myself. By the time the dice got to me I was the last one left at the table, with $28 remaining of my $500. I then proceeded to make seventeen passes, with a fair amount of numbers, and won $15,000.

The same player continued:

> If the original players had remained, the house would have been badly hurt. Not one player bet while I was shooting except for a young man who

came in about halfway through my roll and played
with $5 chips and won about $200.

During the roll, I made three elevens for the
dealers at $25 a pop. This made me very popu-
lar with them and they were really rooting for me.
I believe the roll could have been longer if my wife
hadn't come over to ask, "How are you doing?"
This to me was the kiss of death.

Let me tell you of an experience of mine. Same casino. Nearly nine years later.

It was New Year's Eve at Caesars Palace—or rather,
about 5 A.M. New Year's Day. I walked from one dice
table where I had just lost my self-disciplined limit for
that table to another table where as the shooter tossed
the dice and they were still in the air I called "$75 com-
ing" and the dealer instinctively replied: "Bet."

But then he directed my attention to the little sign in
front of him that read: Minimum bet, $100.

"There goes your three-unit system," the dealer said.

He was correct. My play is always to bet three units
on the line so that I can get maximum free odds behind
the line.

I stood still. I hadn't been doing well and wasn't eager to bet blacks ($100 chips) instead of greens ($25
chips). But while I was thinking about it, the young
man to my right kept throwing number after number. I
became aware that I was in the middle of a good shoot.
I sprang into action. On and on he went, making numbers and making points. It was a beautiful shoot and by
the time he sevened out I was a winner for the trip.

The dice were passed to me.

"I'm a hard act to follow," the young man said.

"You sure are," I said.

I put three black chips on the line. And I was off and
running.

Midway in my hand, someone at the other end of the

table called "eleven" and flung a white ($500) chip to the stickman. I threw an eleven.

"Same bet," he called, after being paid $7,500.

I threw another eleven.

"Same bet," he called again.

I threw a third eleven.

"Take me down," he said. He'd made profits of $21,000 on three rolls on what is regarded as a sucker bet.

It was the improbable again.

When I sevened out, I left the table. At the cashier's cage a short gray-haired man and his wife approached me.

"I should kiss you," he said.

"Are you the guy with the elevens?" I asked.

"No. But I'm a guy who was a $12,000 loser even after that other fellow's hand, and you turned me into a winner!"

When you think somebody is lucky-streaking, don't just stand there. Do something!

11

Let's talk about dice

This should be a must exercise for anyone who wants to gamble serious money at the dice table.

Obtain a pair of casino dice. You can buy a pair in Vegas novelty shops such as Trader Bill's for $1—or the casino will give you a pair for the asking.

At home, prepare yourself with a nice white sheet of paper and a pencil.

Now toss the dice against your pillow or on the floor against the wall. Record the results.

Throw those dice 36 × 4 or 144 times.

Then study the results.

You're going to be startled. And you're going to have some real understanding of what dice are all about.

There are 36 possible combinations with two dice. If they all turn up, the following will be the results:

2.   (a 1 and a 1) will turn up one time.

3   (2 and 1, 1 and 2) will turn up twice.

4. (3 and 1, 1 and 3, 2 and 2) will turn up three times.

5. (3 and 2, 2 and 3, 4 and 1, 1 and 4) will turn up four times.

6. (3 and 3, 4 and 2, 2 and 4, 5 and 1, 1 and 5) will turn up five times.

7. (6 and 1, 1 and 6, 5 and 2, 2 and 5, 4 and 3, 3 and 4) will turn up six times.

8. (4 and 4, 6 and 2, 2 and 6, 5 and 3, 3 and 5) will turn up five times.

9. (6 and 3, 3 and 6, 5 and 4, 4 and 5) will turn up four times.

10. (5 and 5, 6 and 4, 4 and 6) will turn up three times.

11. (6 and 5, 5 and 6) will turn up twice.

12. (6 and 6) will turn up once.

This is elementary for most readers, but be patient with this sole gesture to the uninitiated.

Those possible combinations are what make for dice odds.

7 will come up 6 times to the 5 times that a 6 or 8 will come up so the true odds are 6 to 5.

7 will come up 6 times to the four times that a 5 or 9 will come up so the true odds are 6 to 4 or 3 to 2.

7 will come up 6 times to the three times that a 4 or 10 will come up so the true odds are 2 to 1.

Over any extended period of play the house will grind the player out because it has an advantage of 1.41 percent on the "Do" side and slightly less on the "Don't" side.

If you record 144 throws of the dice, your results should be remarkable in their resemblance to the proper odds. Four should come up 3 times 4 or 12 times. And so forth.

What should this teach you?

Namely, that the numbers do tend to come up their respective number of times and only their sequence varies, and your hope is to catch the right sequence.

Analyze your 144 throws as if you had been betting with the shooter. Now analyze them as if you were a don't bettor. Then analyze them following the "three is a trend" philosophy so that if three shooters didn't make a pass, you switch to "Don't pass."

If you aren't willing to do this little exercise, then you should stay clear of the dice table.

I did the exercise for you. But looking at my scoreboard isn't going to teach you much emotionally. You've got to do this yourself.

Here is the sequence in which my dice tosses came up:

7	11	8	7	4*
8	11	11	8	3
4	2	6	6*	9
8*	10*	8	6	6
2	5	8	12	7
10	7	7	4	6
9	8	6	9	6*
6*	5	7	7	7
8	3	6	6	8
3	9	5	9	4
4	6	7	9	4
10	7	4	6	8
11	11	11	7	11
9	12	7	11	9
5	3	9	5	7
4*	6	4*	4*	8
12	7	9	8	3
9	12	9	7	11
3	5	6	5	5

10*	4*	6	7	11
8*	3	10*	5	5
8	7	5	6	9
10	9	10	6	5
6*	5	4	5	7
7	6	11	4	5
10	2	3	11	7
9	6	12	7	8
7	6	6	7	10
8*	5	9	5	(8) Extra roll to complete the hand

— Decision roll
* Hard-way roll

What do you glean from this showing?

Well, the shooter would have won 20 hands (including the last, for the dice came 8 on the 145th roll) and lost 23. However, if he'd been on the don't side he'd have won only 20 of the bets in view of the "Bar 12" rule.

There was a decision every 3 3/7 rolls.

Now, here is how the numbers came up against probabilities:

Number	Should Have Come Up	Came Up
2	4	3
3	8	8
4	12	13
5	16	17
6	20	22
7	24	23
8	20	16
9	16	16
10	12	9
11	8	12
12	4	5
	144	144

Hard ways (two of the same number) should have come up 4 times each, for a total of 16 hard ways.

They came up 15 times.

2-2 should have come up 4 times.   Came up: 5
3-3 should have come up 4 times.   Came up: 4
4-4 should have come up 4 times.   Came up: 3
5-5 should have come up 4 times.   Came up: 3

A final observation: probability is a prediction, based on mathematics, of what *may* happen. It doesn't mean it *must* happen or that it always will happen.

Don't settle for what you've just read.

Do it yourself.

12

Introduction to money management

Before you walk to the dice table—or the baccarat table—it's time to assimilate guiding Rule Five.

This one is so simple and obvious that if you have ever done any real gambling it will seem like kindergarten instructions.

PUT LIMITS ON POSSIBLE LOSSES FOR EACH BOUT—
AND STICK TO THEM

Let us say that your total stake is $3,000. Before you walk to the table, fix firmly in your own mind your maximum initial loss. Let's say you decide on $300. You may, if you wish, mentally fix another $200 as a reserve.

If chance isn't going your way and you lose $300 but you have the feeling (the feeling, not the hope) that things will change and you are more in tune with what's happening, risk the other $200. If that goes, *walk*.

If you can't obey this discipline, then the following is true:

1. You can't control yourself and have no place in a casino playing with real money. Stay home and play Monopoly instead.
2. You don't *really* want to win.

Now, this book is not intended to be a psychology primer or a self-help guide to knowing yourself. But this question is the key to everything.

Do you really want to win?

Silly? Not at all. You would be amazed at what motivates most people in their gambling. And you would be amazed at how many feel clean and comfortable after losing but terribly uncomfortable when they are winning.

Clean? Yes, clean! You've heard the expression, "I took a bath."

Think about it. DO YOU REALLY WANT TO WIN?

Placing limits on your gaming at any table is the certain indicator of how much control you have over yourself. Keep reminding yourself that THE CONTEST IS BETWEEN YOU AND YOURSELF AND NOT YOU AND THE CASINO.

And keep reminding yourself that you're there not to play but *to win*.

Ask yourself if you really want to win and then sit quietly and let your true feelings surface. What *is* that feeling? Is the answer "yes" or "I don't know" or "not really" or "no"?

If the answer is YES and you genuinely want to leave Las Vegas with more money than you had on arrival, you've got to pay some dues.

You've got to constantly remind yourself that YOU ARE NOT IN THE CASINO TO ENJOY YOURSELF. The pleasure of profits should be enjoyment enough for you: Let others have the fun at the games.

You aren't there to play games, see shows, eat good

food or lounge in royal suites. All of that is for the puppy dogs and the pussy cats. All of that is the chloroform that will make the separation of man and his money as painless as possible.

Reread the above paragraph. It is so critical—so valuable—it should be printed in gold leaf.

13

A positive approach to craps

Let's get into your actual dice play.

By now you have tossed the dice 144 times at home, made a record of the results and studied them. You also are totally familiar with odds.

Before you bet Dollar One, be sure you know and understand the house rules. Ask questions. What is the casino's maximum bet? Its minimum? Does the house allow double odds?

Okay, let's talk about odds.

I mentioned earlier that my play is to place three units* on the line. When a number becomes a point, I take the full free odds.

I play with three units because that allows me maximum free odds. The free (true) odds bet is the only break-even bet the casino offers you.

In theory, over an extended period of time neither

---

*$1, $5, $25, $100, $500—the level of your play doesn't matter. It's 3 of whatever value chips you're betting.

you nor the casino is supposed to benefit by the wager. It's a break-even. In reality, this is one place where, when you are running right, you can make the most profit for your risk.

With 3 units on the line: if you throw a 4 or 10 you put 3 units behind the line and these pay 2 to 1.

With 3 units on the line: if you throw a 5 or 9 you put 4 units behind the line and these pay 3 to 2.

With 3 units on the line: if you throw a 6 or 8 you put 5 units behind the line and these pay 6 to 5.

In every case you can be sure of your payoff because the payoff is always 9 units.

What then are double odds?

A few years ago a young fellow named Bill Friedman saw that he couldn't beat the odds himself so he decided to become a management expert. He taught courses at the University of Nevada on how to run a casino. These were well attended.

Then he wrote a book for me.* He told me the book's publication opened the door to a casino manager's job with the Howard Hughes organization. He went to work for the Summa Corporation, managing its stiff: a small place called the Castaways. Small? It has, for example, a single dice table. (And the unluckiest table in Las Vegas for me!)

No fancy showroom. No gourmet dining room. Not even a lounge show. How then to attract players?

Are you ready? He built a parking lot. *A parking lot!* Its advantage is that you park your own car and walk directly from the lot into the casino. No valet tips. No long walks. No lobbies to lumber through.

But Bill Friedman did more than that. He announced a high payoff on slot machines and free *double odds* on dice.

Others watched closely as Friedman turned the Cast-

Casino Management by Bill Friedman. $40.00. Published by Lyle Stuart Inc.

aways into the most profitable-per-dollar-invested casino in the Hughes collection of seven. Now he also manages the Silver Slipper. That's two. Someday he may run all of the Hughes casinos.

What are free double odds?

You understand why my line bets are 3 units? In an ordinary game, you bet 3 units on the line. You know now (but it's worth repeating) that if you throw a 4 or 10, you back it up with 3 units; a 5 or 9 with 4 units and a 6 or 8 with 5 units.

With double odds you can back a 4, 5, 9 or 10 with 6 units and (in most double odds casinos) a 6 or 8 with 7½ units.

This is what it means in payoffs:

4 or 10. You bet 3 on the line and 6 behind. If your number comes up before a 7, you are paid a total of 24 units for a profit of 15. You get back the 3 you bet on the line plus even money for that part of the winning bet. You get back the 6 you bet behind the line plus the true 2 to 1 odds of another 12 units.

And so forth for the other numbers.

At first I was skeptical. The access to free double odds meant that the house was cutting its percentage from 1.41 to .6. Why should they do that?

One reason might be to induce you to bet more money and so to knock you out of the box more rapidly. There is a theory that the less time a player stands at a table, the less chance he has to catch a streak. (I don't happen to buy this one.)

I went to Friedman and asked him for the casino philosophy.

"Purely competitive," he explained. "If every casino did it we'd lose our edge."

What it means, of course, is that if you bet a series of winning bets you'll win much more money much more quickly. But if you lose, you'll lose more money more quickly, too.

Your choice.

Want to know mine? I now give 90% of my dice play where they offer double odds.

Here is one part of my play that is rigid. I never make a bet unless I have the dollars and the determination to back it with fullest available free odds. If you don't do this, you are giving the house too much of an edge against you and you might as well quit now.

Repeat: Never make a line bet or a come bet that you are not willing and able to back up with full odds.

If you lose your nerve because the results seem to be going against you, walk away from the table. Give yourself a chance to build your resolve by doing something else for a while.

Why should you care about maximum bet limits? I'll give you the reason right here.

Sometime, when things are not going well with you and you seem to be getting ground out, you might want to make one larger wager to see if in a single win you can recover your losses.

It's a bold move. But no more dangerous than standing still while you are being ground down.

Also, sometime you might get lucky and, while lucky, you may want to press your luck. You should know in advance where the ceiling is.

At the moment it's $3,000 at Binion's Horseshoe Club on Fremont Street. With $6,000 free odds. (Though if you arrange with them first, your limit can be as high as the amount of your first wager—whether it be $10,000 or $40,000.)

The Aladdin offers $2,000 maximum bets with $4,000 in free odds. Among others with free double odds are the Dunes and the Stardust.*

I have heard intelligent men like Dr. Arnold Boston (a dentist and one of the best card men in the world)

---

*It's difficult to spell out specific information in a book because rules and limits are subject to overnight change. I offer a few examples, but check 'em out before you go into action.

argue that double odds do not change percentages and are, in fact, an illusion.

It depends on how you look at it. In theory, free single or double odds are an even-money bet against the house. In theory, in the long run neither of you will win any money on it.

But let's examine it in simple practical dollar terms. Let's say you have $30 to bet. You bet it on the line and throw a 4 (or 10). No free odds. You will make the 4 (or 10) once in three hands and lose it twice.

Wager: $90. Return: $60.

Instead you bet $15 on the line, throw 4 (or 10) and take $15 odds. Again, you will win only once in three hands. But you receive two to one for your odds money.

Wager: $90. Return: $75.

Now, instead, you play taking double free odds.

You bet $10 on the line, throw a 4 (or 10) and take $20 double odds. You will win, on average, the same one in three hands.

Wager: $90. Return: $80.

You're wagering the same amount of money in all cases but on, for example, the particular point of 4 (or 10) you come away with $60 on a line no-odds bet and $80 on a line with double odds bet.

Agreed that you won't take down as much money on a come out roll of 7 or 11 or lose as much on a 2, 3, or 12. But that isn't the thrust of the bet. The wager cuts down house percentage against you on that particular bet from 6 to 3 (2 to 1) to 5 to 3.

Now let's talk about the contest between reality and superstition.

Most dice players will repeat some of the things I have spoken about earlier: belief that when dice hit a hand or a die jumps off the table, there is a likelihood that the next roll will be 7-out.

I, too, believed things like that. For years.

One day I decided to find out. I was curious about whether the belief came about because one is vividly aware of hunches that come true but quickly forgets them when they don't. I started to keep records.

Sevens should come up an average of once in six rolls.

I observed that hitting a hand or bouncing onto the floor had no statistical effect on the number of times 7 came up on the next roll. You can forget that. If, on the other hand, you feel comfortable taking off your odds and everything else that will come off after a die goes off the table, etc., by all means do it. Do what you are most comfortable doing.

Observe the loser in action.

He'll make a line bet. That's the good one. He doesn't follow the 3-unit rule because he doesn't take full odds or even understand them.

Now he'll throw money for "c & e" (craps and eleven) or "any craps"! As soon as a point is thrown, he'll cover the hard ways.

He's a dice desperado and his good 1.41% bet on the line has been drowned in a river of reckless foolishness. His dollars* are headed for the waterfall that will carry them into the casino counting room.

Once in a while he'll feel glamorous hitting a long shot on the center layout play. But the good runs there are soon swallowed by the jaws of averages, and he'll go away blaming his run of bad luck.

Casino managers love you to make proposition bets. There is nothing puzzling about this. Proposition bets give the house a greater advantage against you than line bets.

Don't be angry with them. If they could persuade you to mail your check to them without coming to town, I'm sure they'd be happy that they didn't have to go through the motions in order to take your money.

Proposition bets are sucker bets. Let's take the exam-

---

*Very often I talk in terms of dollars rather than chips. Changing chips for your dollars is the anaesthetic they give you— the first step on the way to cutting you up.

ple of the bet on any craps that will pay you 7 to 1.
Let's say that I have $300 on the line. I bet an additional $50 on "any craps." The dice come out and total
2, 3 or 12. Craps! I lose my $300 line bet. The stickman instructs the dealer to give me $350. My original
$50 bet is now working on the next roll. (If I take it
down, I have a flat $50 profit.)

Sounds good, right?

Except that "any craps" will come up only once in
eight times. If you make the bet consistently and the
numbers come up in proper probability over any period
of time, you will pay $1,800 and receive in return a
total of $1,600.

This means you will lose an average of $200 if you
make the wager 36 times.

Odds against you: 11.11%.

Is it any wonder that the dealer keeps intoning,
"Make a bet on craps."

Are proposition bets ever worthwhile?

Sure.

Mannie Kimmel used to beat proposition bets in an
interesting way. He had little counting machines in each
pocket. He'd stand patiently by, clocking a long series
of dice rolls until one number didn't show up for a
while. He favored 2's, 11's, and 12's.

When one of those hadn't come up in a long time (as
for example, in 40 rolls) he began betting that number
every roll. When it failed to come up in another 30
rolls, he would increase his bet. Rarely did he fail to
walk away with a profit. Most of us don't have that
kind of patience.

Mannie was brilliant when it came to odds. One day
he walked into a Las Vegas sports book establishment
and looked at the odds they offered against each of the
National League baseball teams making second place.
He immediately made a $2,000 wager on every team.
He had spotted a fallacy in the house mathematics: no
matter who won, he'd show a profit.

The house knew Mannie Kimmel and immediately after his wager, the odds were studied and changed.

In this case the bookies were right in making their change. Many times, however, when someone approaches the action in an unusual way, they become very concerned. They not only want to see what you're doing; they want to understand *why* you're doing it.

I'm reminded of this bit of gambling humor:

Asylum inmate to psychiatrist: "I'm a gambler."

Shrink: "Fine. You can gamble here."

"With whom?"

"Well, that fella over there is a bookie. . . ."

"With what?"

"We use little stones from the driveway," said the shrink.

So the gambler went to the driveway. but instead of picking up pebbles he shouldered a boulder and carried it to the bookie.

"I want to make a bet with you," he said.

"Oh, no," said the bookie.

"Why not?" asked the gambler.

The bookie pointed to the boulder:

"If you want to bet *that* big, you must *know* something!"

Back to serious business.

Watch this happen again and again at the table: A man will place a number. The number is thrown.

"Press it," he says. Most of his profits are added to the place bet.

It comes in again.

"Press it," he says.

When it's all over he, too, walks away wondering why he has such poor luck.

What in the world was he waiting for? Even the most imaginative day-dreamer among dice players doesn't fantasize about a hand in which the shooter will never ever ever again roll a seven!

Does the man who keeps saying "press it" and "press it" *really* want to win? Think about it.

I often approach the dice table from the opposite point of view. I don't have any more control of the cubes than the next fellow except that I don't pick 'em up so that the numbers on top or on the side facing me are numbers I don't want.

I throw a point. I take full odds behind my line bet. If I am flush with casino winnings or feeling very positive about things, I may not only make a "come" bet with three units, but I may put (place) $300 on each of the other numbers.

I buy rather than place the 4 and 10—paying 5% or $15 on $300—and place the others. It doesn't pay to buy the others and it does to buy 4 and 10. Buying means that if that number comes in I will receive true (2 to 1) odds on my bet rather than 9 to 5.

Let's take a moment to explain how place bets are paid off. I meet veteran crap shooters who don't understand it.

When you place a number, the first unit you place will be paid off at even money. The other units will be paid at true odds.

For example, you place five chips on "5." A "5" is thrown. You get one chip for your bottom chip and the other four are paid off at 3 to 2 or 6 more chips. True odds on a "5."*

Back to my action. With every number covered, I have to hope that I start throwing numbers.

*6 or 8 pays even money on the first chip and 6 to 5 on the others for a payoff of 7 to 6. True odds are 6 to 5. 5 or 9 pays even money for the first chip and 3 to 2 on the others for a payoff of 7 to 5. True odds are 7½ to 5. If you place 4 or 10 you get even money for the first chip and 2 to 1 on the others for a payoff of 9 to 5. True odds are 2 to 1. House percentages are 1.51 on 6 or 8; 4.00 on 5 or 9 and 6.66 on 4 or 10. Thus it is always wise to place the others and buy (for 5%) the 4 and 10.

When I throw a number, I call "down with odds."

That means that my place (or buy) bet is paid off and the original bet and the profits are given to me except for the amount of money necessary to get full odds on my "come" bet, which is now moved to the same number. I make a new "come" bet.

Let's take the example of "10" which I have covered with a $300 "buy" bet.

A "10" is thrown.

I'm paid off at the rate of 2 to 1. $600 for my $300.

My $300 come bet is moved to the 10 box and the dealer keeps $300 for full odds. Of the remaining $600, I rack up $300 and put $300 more on "come."

If 10 comes in again, there is an "on and off" action in theory in which none of the chips are actually moved. "Come" money to the 10 box and odds on the bet. But I am paid 9 units ($900).

Do I stay with this forever?

No. I don't believe in the eternal roll where no 7 ever appears. If I do well, at some point I make a decision to clean the board. I can, if I feel uneasy, call my odds money down and then just worry about the money that went from the "come" box to the numbers.

Or I can simply pick up my last "come" bet so there is nothing on "come." Then, as I roll each number I receive all the "come" wager and the odds wager plus $900 additional in winnings.

You should have learned from your own home education course in tossing dice that those 7's are inevitable. At some point you want to gather as much money into your hands as possible.

Remember that scene at Playboy when I called "odds working"?

The house rule is that odds are off on the come-out roll. I thought about that one. I had a theory, and I wanted to find a fallacy in it. I couldn't.

If having odds on a number is a good bet for the

second roll, why isn't it also a good bet on the come-out roll?

Superstition. Shooters hate to roll a 7 on the come-out and then see all that "come" money and the odds money get taken away by the dealer—even while the shooter wins his line bet.

So what? Is it any less painful if he rolls a 7 on the second roll when the odds *are* working?

My own instinct (with rare gut-hunch exceptions) is to call "odds working" on every come-out roll. I win some, and I lose some. It hasn't been a bad bet at all. The reason the casino is content with the rule that odds are off on the come-out roll is that the odds bet is not profitable so why encourage it more than necessary?

Incidentally, if the house won't lose money on a true odds bet, why not allow you triple or even unlimited true odds behind your line bet?

The answer is easy. If they allow you triple odds then you would tend to bet less money on the line (where the house has a 1.41 percentage against you) and more money on true odds where the house has no advantage at all.

I happen to be very conscious of which numbers do and don't show up. For example, if I have placed or bought all the numbers and by the time I 7-out everything but the 9 has come in at least once, I'm likely to place the 9 after the next shooter throws a point. If it doesn't show up with him, I'll increase my wager.

Probability says that 9 should come up. We also know that it's possible that one won't come up for a half-hour. Unlikely but possible.

Assuming a normal run of numbers, I consider it a good bet.

I'm also conscious of 7's. When a large number of 7's have come up in a short time, I remember my exercise at home. 7 is only supposed to come up once in six rolls. If there have been six 7's in fifteen rolls, it could mean that somebody may be about to throw a spate of numbers before another 7 shows its face.

Remember, too, that the improbable does happen. I watched a player throw eight consecutive craps. I watched another throw six 4's in a row.

It's mid-morning on a holiday weekend. The joint is jumping. The fellow to my right is playing with $500 (white) chips. He bets eight chips ($4,000) on "don't" and then lays full odds after any number is thrown. Obviously they've given him special limits because he has as much as $10,000 going against the shooter making his point.

I watch him win hand after hand.

The dice come to him and he passes and the dice come to me.

"Be careful," I tell him. "I sometimes shoot a powerful hand."

He smiles.

I roll a number. Then lots of other numbers, but never the point.

He wins against me, too.

There aren't many players at the table. Twice more the dice come around and twice more I can't make my point.

The fellow to my right has winnings in excess of $90,000.

Nobody has asked me, but I remark: "Were I you, I'd get on the next plane home."

He smiles enigmatically. No comment.

I leave.

Hours later I pass the table. He's still at it. His beard has begun to grow in. He appears weary. The pile of white chips in front of him is small.

Hours later he's still there. He's grim. And an obvious loser.

He should have gotten on that plane!

One of my publishing colleagues, Allan J. Wilson,

tells a happier tale. He was on one of the Riviera's bi-annual junket planes from New York and happened to get into conversation with the Chinese couple sitting next to him.

In the course of the flight he learned that they were unmarried, had been traveling companions for several years, and were in the export business.

They said they spent lots of holidays on trips to Las Vegas, the Bahamas, Puerto Rico and wherever else the goddess of chance beckoned.

Although they acknowledged their share of disasters, they insisted that their batting average had been good.

Later, in the casino, Allan Wilson found himself at the dice table shoulder to shoulder with the Chinese couple. They were "fooling around"—making small wagers, taking full odds on line bets and then full odds on their come bets.

Allan went his merry way to another hotel. When he returned at midnight a pit boss he knew told him about the Chinese couple.

According to the pit boss, they'd had a staggering winning run. They'd pyramided their bets to a $154,000 profit.

"What surprised me," said Allan, "was the couple's discipline. They'd cashed in their chips, checked out of the hotel and boarded the last plane of the night for San Francisco, where they planned to enjoy the balance of their holiday."

Allan and I have been in many casinos together. Years ago Mary Louise and I left him at a blackjack table at the Colony Club in London, where the only other player at the table was Telly Savalas.

We returned at 2 A.M. The casino was almost empty. Allan stood at the dice table again with just one other player.

"How are you doing?" we asked.

"They've taken me to the cleaners," he said mournfully. "They've buried me."

"How much?"

"Twenty-five hundred dollars' worth."

We watched a few rolls of the dice and Mary Louise and I both became aware that Allan was doing something *very* wrong. *He wasn't taking odds!*

We joined the game, alternately lecturing him and sometimes grabbing chips out of his hand to bet for him when he protested against putting down full odds.

He threw dice and we threw dice. The minute we took our eyes off him he tended to reduce or omit the odds bet. Again the lecture and the grappling for his chips.

Within an hour he'd won back his losses and was about $1,500 ahead.

I like to think we taught him how to wager at the craps table.

When we returned to New York, Allan gifted us with two pounds of the finest caviar his winnings could buy!

Allan likes to play and stay. I tell him that this means he must be a loser most of the time. He'll confess nothing, but he doesn't put up any argument.

Once, because he had no choice, he *had* to hit and run.

It happened at Del Webb's Sahara. He didn't happen to like the hotel. He didn't like its restaurants. He had a consistent record of losing in the Sahara casino.

This time, however, he had no choice. His companion wanted to see Johnny Carson, who was starring in the Sahara show room. Allan said he had seen enough of Johnny Carson for two lifetimes but his companion wanted to see "if Johnny is as cute and charming" off the TV screen as he appears on it.

You can't argue with a determined woman.

The couple arrived at the Sahara at 11:30 P.M.—

half an hour before show time. Normally he would have been content to be seated and to sip wine.

Allan couldn't bring himself to pass a dice table that was practically deserted. There were two players in action and Allan figured both of them to be shills.*

The shooter had a one dollar chip on the pass line. He rolled an 11.

"Seven got to come after 11," Allan told himself. It doesn't, but it did.

Then the shooter began to make numbers and Allan was with him all the way.

At ten minutes to twelve, Allan's companion tugged at his sleeve. "We'll miss the show," she complained. "We'll miss Johnny Carson."

He cashed in. Because *he had to* and was being dragged away.

Profits for the twenty minutes: $6,600.

"Johnny Carson was funnier than I can ever recall his being before," Allan Wilson says.

Allan is responsible for this amusing report. Being a sucker for gourmet-style restaurants, he frequents the Sands for its Regency Room, the Desert Inn for its Monte Carlo Room, and so forth.

He was in the Sands casino at 3 A.M. one morning after a hearty dinner and show. The dice table was crowded but two wrong bettors were having the best of it.

You know the pattern. The shooter throws a number. His point is 9. He tosses two other numbers and then the inevitable "7-out, a loser."

Allan watched the action for ten minutes without risking a sou. He was waiting for the dice to pass him by.

He was to be the next shooter when suddenly a schol-

---

*He was probably wrong. Although Fremont Street casinos use shills to get a dice game started, Strip casinos usually do not, except at the baccarat tables.

arly looking gentleman stepped up to the table to his right.

He apologized and asked if Allan minded if he picked up the dice first. Since Allan hadn't been playing and intended to pass the dice anyway and bet wrong against the subsequent shooter, he smiled and moved to the left to make more room for him.

He bet wrong. The man's first roll was a 7.

He bet wrong again and the man threw another 7.

It was very disconcerting. Then came that infinite moment in time which all gamblers experience.

Let Allan tell it in his own words from here on:

"Call it intuition, prescience, *déjà vu*, or what have you, I *knew* that this man was about to have a great roll.

"I put money on the line. He rolled an 8. Not a bad point. I took full odds behind the line, placed all the other numbers and made a come bet.

"Believe it or not, the shooter held the dice for thirty-eight minutes. He defied every law of probability. He didn't throw his 8 but he didn't throw another 7. He just threw number after number after number.

"Most of us stood there not quite believing what we were witnessing.

"Suddenly the dice came up 8, the point. A loud cheer went up, for by now everyone around the table had gotten onto the roll and the cage was sending out container after container of chips.

"Now he threw three craps in succession.

"My intuition again stood me in good stead. I took down everything that I could take down. He threw a 5 and then sevened out.

"Starting with a few hundred dollars I had worked up a stake of just under $7,000.

"The shooter had done just about the same.

"The pit boss said to him, 'You should have won a hundred grand with a roll like that!'

"The fellow merely smiled and said, 'I didn't want to hurt you.' "

A word about casino dice. Casino craps are called "bank craps" because the casino banks the game and you can bet with or against the shooter.

A pair of dice may cost you $20,000 but they cost the casino less than $2. Dice are manufactured to an accuracy of 1/10,000th of an inch. This is about 1/20th of the thickness of a human hair.

When I was a tentative point holder in the Aladdin, one of its casino executives, Jimmy Konys, would sometimes present a heavy loser at the dice table with a pair of gold dice with the player's name printed on them.

The owner of the gold dice invariably went home, showed them around, and boasted that he'd received them because "I rolled such a long hand."

Perhaps if he told the story often enough he would believe it himself. And remember, Konys gave the gold dice *only* to losers!

Some years ago I knew a fellow whom I'll call Billy G. Billy was a successful businessman in Phoenix, Arizona. He owned a number of shops including one at the airport. He had a lovely wife.

Billy was a dice degenerate. He went for his cash. He went for his checks. He went for markers. He went very broke.

His wife divorced him.

One day he sat in a plane in Cleveland waiting to take off. The plane exploded on the runway and sixty people were killed. But eight passengers in the rear section (including an infant) were blown safely out of the plane. Billy was one of the lucky eight.

Billy never set foot in a plane again.

To get to Las Vegas from Phoenix by train or automobile is quite a trip. Billy made it frequently.

One day at the Royal Nevadan, Billy got lucky at the

craps table. When he was ready to cash in, he was an $80,000 winner.

There was consternation in the cashier's cage and an interminable delay as he stood waiting to receive his eighty grand.

Finally he was invited into the executive offices. "Mr. G.," he was told, "I'm embarrassed to say that at the moment we don't have the cash in the cage to pay you off, but maybe there's something else we can work out."

After much conversation, Billy was offered two shop locations in the hotel rent-free for eighteen months. He said he'd think about it and accepted a receipt for his $80,000. Then he phoned Phoenix and asked his accountant to fly to Las Vegas.

The accountant arrived and pored over the casino records. "The place can't last, Billy," he said. "Certainly not for eighteen months."

Billy G. thought about it. "Well, something is better than nothing," he announced, and accepted the offer.

Six months passed and Billy recouped his eighty thousand, and then some, on the two hotel lobby shops. He was summoned to Las Vegas.

He made the long journey. Once again he was invited into the executive offices. "Billy, you've got an interest in this place so I thought I should tell you that we're going to have to fold in about ten days."

Twenty thousand dollars in chips were pushed toward him.

"Take these. Spread 'em around town. Do it quickly."

In those days the chips of any casino were cashable at every other casino in town. Banks and merchants accepted them as money and made change for them— often with silver dollars.

Billy spread the chips around by playing against them at other casino dice tables. He did okay for himself.

A week later the Royal Nevadan closed its doors. It

was bankrupt. Its chips were worthless and those who held them were stuck with them.

Years have passed. Billy still makes the tiresome trip to Las Vegas. Still plays Bank Craps. Is a constant loser.

Incidentally, casino winnings are not legally collectable and should a casino close because of financial difficulties, you do not go on the list of creditors. Your claim cannot be processed through the courts.

It works in reverse too, of course. Gambling debts are not legally collectable from the player.

Nevertheless, most losers pay their debts. Less than four percent of all credit extended by the casino results in bad debts. This, despite the fact that as much as 50% of the income of some casinos is based on credit. (The I.R.S. does not require the casino to consider winnings as income until they've been collected.)

Credit investigation systems are quite sophisticated. Take, for example, the Las Vegas Hilton. A file is kept of all persons who have ever requested credit. The customer's card contains such information as his junket history, how his markers have been paid, whether they're paid at the tables, the cage, or whether he left town owing money. In addition to indicating his credit limit, the card rates him as a player. Many players are rated by two casino executives in the pit each time they play.

At Caesars Palace, where 50% of the play depends on credit, credit markers consist of four stubs which are divided into six stubs each. At any time it is possible to account for all the markers. A computer system monitors 70,000 active credit cards and another 50,000 inactive ones. The casino is plugged into the central credit bureau so that it can monitor your action, credit line, and money owed at other casinos in town.

Recently, a middle-aged fellow with moustache and Spanish accent walked up to the dice table where I stood playing. He dropped four white ($500) chips on

Field—one of the worst wagers on the casino craps lay-out.*

The field bet being a sucker's bet, it is often called a "ladies' bet" because it depends on the innocent patsy to put money in that nice big space that pays off when the shooter rolls a 2, 3, 4, 9, 10, 11 or 12. Even with a 2 to 1 payoff on 2 and 12, you will win 18 chips and lose 20 chips if you bet a chip on every roll.

So here, before my very eyes, was a man betting $2,000 on one of the worst bets on the table.

What followed were a series of 2's and 12's and 3's and 9's and 11's. Within minutes he was $20,000 ahead.

"It owes me this," he said. "They really put it to me at the baccarat table last night!"

The dice come to me. I wish he would quit. He doesn't. I throw a 6. Then an 8. Then I 7-out. Cost to him: $6,000.

He plays on, but I move away. I don't want to witness the massacre.

If you've been at enough tables, you've seen it in variation. An improbable series of lucky wins. But the player has no goals, no discipline, no ability to quit winners. Soon enough he will quit losers.

Don't let it be you.

---

*The house has an advantage ranging from 5.263 percent to 11.111 percent depending on whether or not it offers double on 2 or 12. That's not as bad as proposition bets like "any 7" or 2, 3, 11 or 12—all of which give the house 16.666 percent.

14

More advice on dice

Mannie Kimmel used to insist to me that it wouldn't matter if a monkey threw the dice.

If you feel that way, you are ideally and temperamentally suited to gambling.

However, if you, like myself, are affected by your impression of the person throwing the dice, don't hesitate to go with your instinct and your intuition. You may be wrong, but I've made the point before that you should be as comfortable as possible in what you are doing.

If you take an intense dislike to the guy at the other end because he appears to be an anal character smoking a stinking cigar, my advice is stand by and not bet. You're not going to be happy betting with him. And if you are suckered by your response into betting against him, you're playing emotional dice and losing control and perspective.

On the other hand, occasionally you'll watch someone pick up dice and you'll have a strong positive feeling. It's worth taking a larger-than-usual chance. Play hunches. There's nothing wrong with it. You'll be right often and wrong often.

I have played some far-out hunches when I held the dice. For example, I will occasionally call a proposition bet that isn't even on the table a hopping bet. I call a number in exactly the way I believe it will fall. Thus, I don't say "6" but rather "4 and 2 on the hop."

It's a one-roll wager, and I lose if any other number comes up or even if "6" comes up any other way.

Some years ago when *Life* published a rather silly article about me, they had two paragraphs about my gambling which read:

Back at the crap tables, the dice came to Stuart and something eerie happened. He began to glow. Call it a hallucination, a trick played by the casino lights—I saw it and so did the man standing next to me. Stuart suddenly began to glow like a filament charged with current. He was going to have a streak. The pit boss appeared quickly from nowhere. "A Lyle Stuart streak," he told me later, "is one of the spectacles of gambling. In five minutes, counting side bets, he can take the house for a hundred grand." Stuart can't explain how it happens. All he knows is that for four or five minutes he knows exactly what the dice or cards are going to do.

He stared at the dice now, bright red against the dark green table. Patted them, smacked them, fussed with them as a mother fusses with a baby. Suddenly he snapped them up and flung them the length of the table. "5 and 2!" he yelled while the dice were still in the air; 5 and 2 came up. The whole table gasped. Once more Stuart fidgeted with the dice and then flung them. "Hard 6!" he yelled. Two 3s showed. The table was in an uproar. Next, he called 11 and made it. Then 4. Then 9. The crowd stood three-deep. Men were *yelling, women squealing. Dealers were paying bets as fast as their hands could move. In five minutes he won back $31,000.*

As with most of the rest of the article, it was apple-sauce. But it brings up the subject of precognition and ESP.

Do I believe in any god or gods or supernatural destiny? No. I'm an atheist from way back.

If you believe there is some god or gods watching over you, more power to you and your imagination. From Thomas Edison to Albert Einstein, the most knowledgeable scientists of our time—and those who best understood how the universe works—discarded the idea of a personal deity.

So you believe this giant IBM machine in the sky is going to look down on you (among its three billion subjects) and care whether you make a 6 or 7?

Good for you.

I tend to go along with crusading journalist George Seldes in that I believe nothing I hear and only half of what I see.

I don't know the explanations for everything, but I do know that there *are* explanations. I don't believe human beings are at the end of the road in learning about things that happen on the earth on whose crust we live.

With that as prelude, let me say that it is only at gambling that my senses have been so acute on occasion that I have had mystical experiences. Nothing supernatural, but flashes for which I do not yet have the explanation.

Let's backtrack for a moment. If you are of my generation, you're familiar with the Rodgers and Hart song "Where or When," in which "some things that happen for the first time, seem to be happening again."

We've all had that experience, that feeling. It's called *déjà vu.* We've also all had hunches, and then the hunches came true and on some occasions it was chilling.

As regards gaming, you stand at a table and you feel the next roll of the dice will be an 8 or 7 or an 11— whatever. *And it happens that way!* Wow! It's all very vivid and you recall it for the rest of the day and the day after, too.

What you don't remember . . . what you tend to immediately blank out of memory . . . are those hunches that *don't* come true. The man or lady picks up the dice. "Oh, oh," you tell yourself, "it's gonna be 7-out."

The next roll is a 10.

You completely forget the hunch.

Being aware of this and of the occasional (sometimes only once in four days, sometimes four times in two days) streaks of foreknowledge I believed I had, I decided to test myself to put to rest once and for all this peculiar feeling that my mind was racing ahead of time.

What I did was have someone accompany me. When I got that premonition, I told my companion in a quiet voice what was coming up. I didn't say merely "8" but rather "5 and 3." Not 4 but "3 and 1."

The feeling came upon me the second day. *I called eleven consecutive rolls of the dice exactly right!* On the twelfth roll I said "two aces" and the dice rolled a 2 and a 1.

I have had similar (though not as extended) experiences at baccarat. I've known exactly what my cards were before turning them over. On a sample occasion (when I was dealing from the shoe) the player showed an 8.

That's okay," I announced with complete confidence, "I've got a 2 and a 7 of spades." And that's what I turned over.

I'd then call the next few cards dealt to Player and to Bank exactly right.

It has worked in reverse, too. Betting on Player, I've

turned over an 8, and when someone nearby remarked, "Good," I've replied, "No good. The bank has a 9."

And indeed it did.

Are there explanations? Of course. I'm not a magician or a mind reader. I'm not a sage or a clairvoyant. But this thing at the dice table has happened to me again and again.

I've speculated that perhaps I've been standing at dice tables so long over a twenty-one-year period that my mind has become a computer with some recognition of what should come up because it hasn't come up.

I don't know. When it happens I don't fight it: I go with it.

If you're tired, walk away. If the smoke from somebody's cigarette bothers you, walk away. If you feel that you're going to be unlucky, walk away. If the stickman moves too quickly for your peace of mind, walk away.

If anything at all bothers you, walk away.

The dice game is as eternal as anything can be in our lifetime. It doesn't end when you walk away. It doesn't begin when you place your first wager.

It's going on all the time. Every day and every night of the year. Now. Even at this moment. Dice are rolling on hundreds upon hundreds of green felt tables, and thousands upon thousands of dollars are being won and lost even as you read this sentence.

You're not losing your last opportunity when you walk away. The game goes on forever. It will go on after you're dead, buried and forgotten.

Relax. There's plenty of time to resume your action.

In the beginning I told you what I thought about systems.

System: A whole composed of parts in orderly arrangement according to some scheme or plan; the set of correlated principles, ideas, or statements belonging to some department of knowledge or belief.

Gamble: Any course involving risk and uncertainty. Dictionary definitions would seem to make the two words, "gambling" and "system," incompatible if not mutually exclusive. Yet gambling systems have existed for centuries.

There is no honest "system" that will consistently beat casino odds. But just to show you one of the paradoxes in gambling, I'll let you in on a "system" that was given to me by one of the major gambling men of our time. (The only thing I won't reveal here is his name.)

Years ago a mutual friend had brought us together because my friend wanted Mr. Gambling Man to dissuade me from gambling.

We spent a pleasant evening in conversation and now we were sitting in a fancy restaurant that was obviously ("secretly") owned by Mr. Gambling Man.

He told me nothing I didn't know. How gamblers are every kind of idiot. How they're every kind of nameless fool. What self-destructive clowns they are.

I frustrated his mission by agreeing completely.

At about 2 A.M. a twinkle appeared in his eye. "I'll show you what assholes gamblers are," he said. "Take you. You say you like craps. Would you risk $2,700 to win $25?"

"Would you repeat that?" I said.

He did.

"Do you think I'm crazy?" I said.

"Of course! Now listen to me. This is the bet. You're going to bet that four consecutive players at the dice table won't make at least four passes each. Once in a long long time you're going to get unlucky and you're going to lose. But generally, you're gonna do fine. Interested?"

I nodded, albeit reluctantly.

He set out the "system."

It consists of a series of wagers. You bet on the "Don't pass" side. You bet $25. If the shooter makes a pass, you bet $50. Then $100. Then $200.

If anywhere along the line he misses, you've made $25. If he makes four passes, you stand back and wish him luck and hope he makes 100 passes: it doesn't affect you. You don't wager again until the dice pass to the next shooter. Then you begin with a new sequence: $50, $75, $150 and $300. If that shooter makes four passes you wait until the dice move to the next shooter. Then the sequence is $75, $100, $200 and $400. The fourth and final sequence is $100, $125, $250 and $500.

As soon as you win a bet you go back to the first sequence.

If four players in a row make four passes or more each, you have lost $2,700.

The odds against it happening are heavy, though I wasn't convinced of that the first time I flew to Las Vegas with the "system" and approached the table with trepidation.

Moving from table to table (I'd move when I'd won $300 to $400 at a table) I found myself with $2,800 in about two hours.

I kept playing this little number on subsequent visits. Sometimes as many as three would make four passes and then it was a while before I was even again. But even I got.

Friends were puzzled when I returned from Vegas a consistent winner.

There are only two pitfalls to that bet.

One is that sometime, and probably when you can least afford it, you're going to lose $2,700. It didn't happen to me but it could have happened and it could happen.

The other and more critical (to me) negative is that it is the dullest way to spend time in a casino that you can possibly imagine. You are a machine, bored silly for hours waiting for outcomes that may take fifteen rolls of the dice before you win or lose $25.

Another factor that affects some people is reluctance

to play on the "Don't pass" side because they think people at the table won't like them.

You're not in Las Vegas to win popularity contests. You aren't playing against the shooter. You're playing against the house. But that isn't enough for some sensitive souls. If playing "Don't" makes you uncomfortable, then *don't*.

Postscript: I once taught this "system" to a friend of mine. Then I watched him at the table.

Whenever the results were going against him, requiring bets like $400, he chickened out. He'd stand there without making a bet. Ironically, again and again on that non-wager the player would 7-out. Or come out with craps. (Keep in mind that only "2" or "3" pay off on the Don't side since "12" is a "push"—you neither win nor lose.)

I should note that this same friend also frequently fails to back up his line bets with odds. I plead with him to cut the initial wager if that's what it takes. But again and again I come upon him not taking advantage of the free odds.

Need I add that on his return from any gambling journey the question is never did he win, but rather how much did he lose?

15

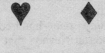

The golden gulch

In 1976, Nevado casinos paid taxes on winnings of $1,400,000,000. Of this, Las Vegas itself reported gaming profits of more than half—$927,000,000.

In 1977, while I was making my ten consecutive winning forays, Las Vegas casinos were showing profit increases of more than 19%.

And that ain't succotash.

Keep in mind that Nevada has had a forty-seven-year monopoly on the casino gaming industry. Oddly enough, the state ranks only sixth in terms of total revenues collected from legal gambling. New York and California earn more from parimutuel wagering alone than Nevada collects from all of its casinos.

The tax on casino earnings ranges from 3 to 5.5 percent.

The casino doesn't pay it. The players do.

Two years ago the Commission on the Review of the National Policy Toward Gambling said that nearly

twenty-eight million tourists came to Nevada in 1975—
nearly a million of whom didn't stay overnight.

Those who stayed did so for an average of three
nights, and spent about $60 a day. Gaming excluded.

Only one-third said that gambling was the main reason they came to Nevada. About as many said the main
attraction was the shows.

The approximately one hundred-fifty small and
medium-sized casinos in Nevada that offer only gaming
produce 3% of the total tax revenue for the state.
Ninety-five percent comes from approximately eighty
casinos. Of these, twenty "super casinos" (most of them
located on the Las Vegas Strip) offer a variety of entertainment, restaurants, garishly decorated rooms, and
lots of recreational features ranging from huge swimming pools to golf courses, tennis courts and sports ex-
hibitions.

You should not be interested in any of it.

They are all there for the people who lose all that
money that pays all those taxes.

If you gamble you are a person who reads more
books, newspapers and magazines than the non-bettor.
You watch less television and go to more nightclubs,
movies and theatres.

Fine. But do all those things in your hometown.

You're in Las Vegas to win.

Okay, why do I talk only in terms of Las Vegas?
What about Monte Carlo? Reno? Macao?

Here I can speak only for myself. I've gambled in
many places. Ranging from casinos in France, with
$10,000 table limits, to Elsinore Castle in Denmark,
where the limit was $2.

To overcome the casino advantage I find my best lo-
cation is Las Vegas. I want to be able to gamble at any
hour of the day or night when I feel like gambling. I
want to be able to move from table to table and from

casino to casino on impulse.* I want to play where my winnings are not critical for the casino.

I also want to gamble when I'm ready for it. I don't want the casino to be located three blocks from where I have my home. Gambling facilities that close would be a danger for me. Going to gamble should require time and effort. A pilgrimage.

Atlantic City doesn't appeal to me, since I live two hours away. The attempt to turn a slum city into a resort town is going to take a sultan's fortune. It will also take as much as ten years for Atlantic City to begin to catch up to Las Vegas. Nor are the Las Vegas gambling bosses concerned. They consider that Atlantic City will be a school—teaching more people how to play the casino games.

Incidentally, have you ever been in Atlantic City in the wintertime? Cold and miserable.

Proximity is dangerous. While only 61% of all adult Americans bet on anything in 1974, 78% of all Nevada residents bet on something that year.

Gambling and crime are closely linked in the public mind.

Las Vegas, for example, does have a high incidence of murder, rape, robbery and burglary compared to the country as a whole. However, its crime rate is no worse than that experienced at other resort areas. It's about the same as Daytona Beach and Fort Lauderdale, Florida.

Tourists make easy targets for robbers, pickpockets, purse snatchers and burglars. One out of every five crime victims in Las Vegas is an out-of-state visitor.

Just knowing this should alert you against carrying large sums of cash on your person when you're roaming

---

*I almost always rent a car because although taxis are always available and their cost reasonable, I want the pleasure of my own campany and a chance to think and plan as I pick the next target.

the streets. Nor is concealing it in the dirty laundry in your hotel room any protection. Hotel keys are like moments of depression: Everybody has them.

Studies have shown that gambling is the heartbeat of organized crime, both locally and nationally.

What about so-called "mob" influence in casinos? Syndicate control became smaller over the years as large corporations took over casino after casino.

Not even Benjamin "Bugsy" Siegel could have imagined anything as spectacular as the MGM Grand, which bills itself as "the world's largest resort hotel." With its 2,100 rooms it can prosper just from the people who occupy its rooms. It needn't seek desperately to attract outside customers.

The "boys" still have their hands in some of the tills. And some of the hands are hidden.

Wouldn't you like to become as lucky as Allen R. Glick? For $22,500 Glick bought a real estate company which happened to be worth $10,500,000.

That's a jackpot win if ever there was one.

Glick was such a nice fellow that the Teamsters Union Pension Fund made loans to him of almost $150,000,000 so that his company (Argent) could own and the control the Stardust, Fremont, Hacienda and Marina.

At this moment a Grand Jury has been investigating hidden mob holdings in the Aladdin.

What does all this mean to you?

Nothing, if whatever happens behind the scenes doesn't pressure employees to cheat you. You need be concerned only with scams which involve cheating the players in order to make up for employee cheating.

According to the Feds, $7,000,000 was embezzled from slot machines in Argent-owned casinos.

Aren't you glad you didn't drop your quarters into any of those slots?

Many casinos have been ripped off by phony junket setups. Junketeers draw chips against markers, play some and cash the rest. The markers are uncollectable. In some cases a scam involves getting the names of people terminally ill. Impostors apply for credit in a $5,000 to $10,000 range, using forged documents of identity.

The casino writes off the debt when the named individual dies.

There are plenty of scam operations involving dealers.

Again, none of these are your problem. If you play in large casinos that have big bankrolls, your goal is solely to win.

Let the Feds worry about the mob influence.

A sample of the kinds of things that happen took place with the Sands. The so-called mob disposed of its interest in the place. Less than two years later, the partners had a falling out and the Sands was sold to Howard Hughes.

The price was so much higher than "the boys" had received for their (hidden ownership) points that word went to the new sellers: "the boys" would like a piece of the pie.

The request didn't come from "the arm" of the Mafia. Rather, it came from Frank Ericson, the gambler's layoff man.

It was not a demand, just a request.

The new sellers decided to accede to the request. "The boys" were given an additional $10,000 a point— or $1,000,000 as a bonus.

Now Howard Hughes was happy, the sellers were happy, and "the boys" were happy.

Less than ten years ago, abstracts published by the Nevada State Gaming Control Board revealed that the return on equity of Las Vegas Strip casinos was 58.5%. Although it is currently between 20 and 30%, that's a lot of profit per dollar invested. To protect those dollars and to insure a steady flow of losers at the tables, the casinos on the Strip spend a lot on their junkets.

Complimentaries for room, food, drinks, entertainment and air transportation cost the hotel about 15% of its operating budget.

Since the casino should win about 20% of the drop (the money dropped into the cash boxes on the tables) then you should be able to gamble $2,500 for the casino to earn back the $500 it spends to bring you to its portals and to house, feed and entertain you.*

If junketeering makes you feel at all obligated to your host casino—if it makes you feel that you "owe them" something—then skip the junket and pay your own way!

You're going to give them a chance at your money and they're going to give you a chance at theirs. But most of the chips are stacked on their side of the table and you don't owe them a thing.

You do owe yourself every opportunity to win their money and to keep it.

Winning, of course, is one thing. Keeping is another.

We've agreed that you aren't a winner until you get your money home.

The mousetrap here is your unwillingness to leave town on the turn of a big win.

There are players who open local bank accounts.† Others buy bank checks and mail them home. Others

---

*The Dunes has set the pace for junkets. It fills planes full of prosperous businessmen. Over the years the casino has, for all practical purposes, become the partner of many a businessman —sharing his profits. The MGM Grand, Caesars Palace, and most of the major casinos run junkets. For example, in 1974 the Hilton ran 144 junkets that brought 14,700 customers to its casino.

†If you deposit cash in a bank you'll have to pay tax on it or show the I.R.S. that you've had equivalent losses. England takes a different view: no income tax is imposed on gambling winnings there.

The I.R.S. guidelines on gambling record-keeping would throw you. They want you to show the date and type of specific wagers. Name and address of the casino. Name(s) of person(s) if any who were there when you played. The hand the money to friends for safekeeping.

For years a running gag in the casino was the husband turning to his wife and saying, "Give me that money I told you not to give me."

You have to work out your own money-escape method. And then you have to stick to it.

---

amount(s) won or lost. The number of the dice table at which you played. Information as to whether credit was issued in the pit or at the cashier's cage. And so forth.

By 1979 the I.R.S. is supposed to report to Congress on whether casino winnings should be subject to withholding.

16

Absent thee from felicity awhile

Charles Kandel was a delightful fellow. Everyone liked him. He was warm, gracious and generous.

In the old days Charlie used to sit on one side of Arnold Rothstein* ("The Big Bankroll") at the front

---

*Rothstein invented the intercity layoff system that insured bookmakers against heavy losses. This marked the beginning of a nationwide illegal gambling apparatus.

He also fixed sporting events. But his claim to notoriety was the introduction of organization to the illegal gambling profession.

World War I and the income tax dampened America's gambling fever but Rothstein was little affected. In 1919, he established a luxurious gambling house in Saratoga.

His criminal career was not limited to gambling interests. He took advantage of the business potential created by Prohibition. He financed retail outlets for bootleggers and provided them with trucks and drivers. He also operated large bail bond and insurance businesses.

Rothstein's addiction to gambling eventually cost him his life. He was shot and killed in 1928 for failing to pay his losses at cards.

table in the old Lindy's restaurant on the east side of Broadway. Jack "Legs" Diamond sat on the other side. The two men were Rothstein's collectors.

Rothstein was, among other nefarious things, a loan shark. He was a "6 for 5" man. You borrowed $5 for one week and paid back $6. That's slightly more than 1,000% annual interest. Better than David Rockefeller will pay you at Chase Manhattan Bank.

The borrower would look into Rothstein's steel blue eyes and say, "Arnold, I'll have this back to you in two weeks," and Rothstein would reply, "God help you if you don't." And there he was, surrounded by those grim looking collectors.

But those were the old days. Before the moustaches found there was more money in legal gambling than in extortion and hijacking. Before they all became gentlemen and churchmen and heads of the local charities.

When it became necessary to gun down the father of it all, Bugsy Siegel, the gunning was done in Beverly Hills.

When it became necessary to stab to death casino owner Gus Greenbaum and his wife, it was done with icepicks in Arizona.

The "boys" had become paragons of virtue.* In their casinos they quickly recognized something the Quakers had learned centuries before: honesty *is* the best policy.

There was no need to cheat at the games. The games were themselves a license to steal. There was no need to be anything but fine gentlemen.

Charlie Kandel became a gentleman.

He set up a scholarship foundation. He was a veteran of more wars than you'd want to remember, and he was active in veteran affairs. Audie Murphy, the most deco-

---

*In Cleveland, Moe Dalitz was a bootlegger and a reputed killer but in Vegas he became the elder statesman of the gaming industry and a very nice fellow. In Detroit, Eddie Levinson paid $1,500 in fines for running a sawdust joint. In Las Vegas he is a wealthy captain of the industry. Etc., etc.

rated hero of World War II, was Charlie's friend. So was Captain Medina, of My Lai massacre notoriety.

Charlie worked at the Sands as an owner. His brother was a Hollywood screenwriter. When Howard Hughes bought the Sands, Charles became "Casino Executive."

He greeted people.

People liked him. He had his own set of ethics and loyalties, and he was true to them. He knew every scam, every form of larceny, every kind of con.

He had his own values. Once, talking about the brother of a rival casino executive, Charlie told me: "You know, Lyle, they put him away on a bum rap."

"Really?"

"Sure.————may have killed five or six guys but he *never* dealt in dope."

Charlie was sincerely indignant at such a miscarriage of justice. Charlie also taught me a rule that I abandoned when I decided to write this book.

"If you want to get rich, get rich in the dark."

IF YOU WANT TO GET RICH, GET RICH IN THE DARK.

There are many reasons for this. There are those who feel that the I.R.S. doesn't play a sportsmanlike game. You can't deduct casino losses, but you are supposed to pay taxes on winnings. Some gamblers consider this rule so unfair they don't.

But reason to operate quietly is that casino owners are as superstitious as most players. They become uncomfortable when you win and win and win. They may not want your business after a while.

Remember that they fire blackjack dealers who run "unlucky" and lose money for the casino.

Remember, too, that they really believe that dice are "hot" or "cold."

Dice are man-made objects with no mind, no memory, no eyes, no nose, no mouth. The only time they become "hot" is when you roast them on a skillet over a lit stove. They can become "cold" if you put them in your refrigerator.

That many casino managers believe dice run "hot" and "cold" only proves that they're almost as crazy as you are for playing their odds-against-you games.

Here is my suggested method of operation that will separate the will-to-winners from the wish-to-winners.

GO TO LAS VEGAS ALONE.

No wife. No girl friend. No companions.

You aren't there for fun and games. You're on a serious mission. It requires all of your concentration.

If you have company, your movements are restricted. You will be spending time in dining rooms and show rooms. You will be talking to your friend at the tables (and thus dissipating your energy and concentration) or eyeing your watch to see when you meet again.

Don't.

And don't tell me about the time you were with a party of eight people and won a lot of money. It's possible. In games of chance, anything is possible.

They tell a story of someone who came to town a few weeks ago and, starting with $80 at the dice table, built a stake of a few hundred thousand at one place, a couple of hundred thousand at another, and so forth, and today is reported to have a cool million on deposit at the Dunes.

Contrast this with the millions upon millions who have lost their bankrolls at dice tables. Sure, one in millions will make that huge killing.

But on balance you want to win on every visit. You must be totally free. To move from table to table and casino to casino. And on impulse to head for the airport to take a plane—any plane to anywhere that will take you away from the action.

If you want fun and games, read no further. This

book won't be of any real help to you. It is written for those few who are determined to win and who understand that they must put aside childish pleasure as part of the admission fee to the winner's circle.

Charlie Kandel died a few years ago. The funeral service took place in New York, and the large room was packed with a mixture of casino owners, managers and players—many of whom had flown cross country for the ten-minute ritual.

He's dead but the wisdom of his words lives on:

**IF YOU WANT TO GET RICH,
GET RICH IN THE DARK.**

To which I add:

—AND DO IT ALONE.

17

The winner's instinct

I'm a big believer in what I call my energy level. This is different from the fatigue level—a subtle difference to be sure, but a difference.

When my energy level is low I know I shouldn't gamble. And yet this is the most critical moment, for when energy is low, resistance is low and discipline tends to erode.

Cards going against you? Stick around; they'll change.

Dice choppy? Eventually it *has* to be different!

Applesauce!

This is the time to run. To your room. Or to the airport. Or to a movie. Or to shop in the Maryland Parkway mall.

But get out of the casino.

The same is true when you're tired. Now, you can be tired from lack of sleep or from the intensity of gambling. But the energy level? Think of yourself as a human battery. You're charged up when you arrive. You concentrate and think and maneuver and suffer and triumph. You're using that mental electricity all the time. When it has been dissipated, it's time to return home and give yourself time to recharge.

As a casino player, you are always bucking a minus computation. Even the most favorable game is really just the least unfavorable.

In the golden days of Damon Runyon there was a fellow named Nicholas Andrea Dandolos. He was better known as Nick the Greek.

In sixty years he is said to have won and lost nearly four hundred million dollars.

I used to watch him at the Sands. He was a *Don't* player at the dice tables. He listened to the stickman's calls but rarely looked at the table. Instead, he stared into the distance across the room.

Don't players die just as broke as *Do* players.* Nick died broke.

But in his halcyon days he was bold (not reckless) and had a fascinating grasp of mathematical odds on any wager.

Nick believed in good judgment and sound instincts. He once said, "When you see a man walk into a casino with an air of quiet confidence and buy a specific amount of chips—without asking whether he can cash a check later should need arise—then proceed directly to one game and test his luck with small wagers until he's sure how it's running, keep an eye on him.

"He will know the game and how it's played *before* he risks his first chip. When he wins, he'll increase his stake, to take full advantage of his luck. And when he's losing, he'll bet conservatively to ride out the streak.

"Should he lose the chips he came in with, he'll quit."

---

*An exception to the "all gamblers die broke" legend is John W. "Bet a Million" Gates. He began as a barbed wire salesman in Texas. He never stopped gambling, winning and losing large fortunes. When he died in 1911 he was worth between $40 million and $50 million.

Nick often remarked that no method known to humanity can change a minus expectation to a plus expectation.

He knew, too, that what often separates winners from losers is attitude. Money management is a test of human character and intelligence. Winning requires the *intention* of winning.

There is something primitive in the human mentality that fears success; the gods get angry if you win too much, and winning big really does scare the average person. Losers feel *safer*, somehow, when they're out of pocket. They've appeased the jealous gods, and feel virtuous because they've taken their lumps, an attitude that goes back to early childhood (mother loves you *after* you've been beaten, everyone is sorry for you when you cry, and no one hates or envies you). Winners stay cool: They have the guts to face the envy and hatred of the losers and the wrath of the gods.

Psychology was part of Nick the Greek's secret. The other part was a carefully thought out method, a "system of plateaus"—for *keeping* some winnings. What it amounted to was this:

Say he started with $500, and hit a winning cycle. He allowed his stake to build, gradually increasing his bets, until he had $1,500. Then he pocketed his original $500 and continued playing with the casino's money. If he lost the thousand, he quit. If he ran it up still higher, $1,000 became his plateau, and the moment he lost back the thousand he quit with the remainder, no matter how much or little it was.

As to his method of increasing wagers, this was largely intuitive with Nick the Greek. Many gamblers say they don't believe in "luck." He did, and he believed, or observed, that it ran in cycles.

Songwriter Irving Caesar (he wrote "Tea for Two," "I Want to Be Happy," and "Just a Gigolo") told me this experience with Nick the Greek. Irving went with Nick to a "high society" party. Downstairs an orchestra played so that some of the season's most widely known debutantes could dance. Upstairs in the master bedroom, a high-stakes dice game took place on the bed.

With sinking feelings Irving watched Nick lose just under $250,000. The game ended and the players straggled downstairs.

"I sat on the bed in a state of shock," Irving reported. "Poor Nick. My friend had just lost a quarter of a million dollars. I was sick over it. I felt awful.

"Finally I dragged myself downstairs. When I raised my head to look at the dancers, there was Nick laughing and dancing with more vigor than anyone on the floor.

"I couldn't believe my eyes. I shouldered my way through the dancers and grabbed his arm. 'For God's sake, Nick! How can you dance? You lost a fortune!'

"He looked at me with surprise, and then with a twinkle of amusement in his eyes. 'Irving,' he said, 'your life doesn't go with it!' "

Nick the Greek also used to say, "The only difference between a winner and a loser is—character."

In this book we call it self-discipline.

WHY DO YOU GAMBLE?

The serious gambler is a man who is at war with Chance and all her bitchy whimsy. . . . In the casino there is, whether he wins or loses, certainty; he consults the table, which speaks to him through the dice, as the Greeks consulted oracles, and the oracle rewards him by telling him now, not next week or next year, whether the choices he is making are right or wrong.
—William Pearson
in his gambling novel,
The Muses of Ruin

18

The bottom line

On my ten consecutive winning trips I did an unusual thing. I carried along my Norelco cassette recorder. After each session at the tables, I talked into it about how I had done and what I had done.

This became a tremendous help to me.

It is amazing to me to listen now to some of the insights (often unintentional) this record provided. In the blur that can set in after too much play, it gave me perspective. It highlighted errors. It showed me what I was doing right. It warned me against repeating errors. It was a constant educational and training process.

That's my thing. Each of us must do his own thing. It works beautifully for me, but might not work at all for you. On the other hand, when you say, "I stayed too long at that table. I have to be more alert about leaving when I'm nicely ahead"—the very act of saying it may alert you to a more disciplined departure in the next round.

Gambling is an esoteric thing. It is a very personal experience. We each see and feel it differently.

In the excitement and when you're in action, it is
sometimes necessary to clarify your goal. It's really very
simple: You want to leave richer than you were when
you arrived.

I know chronic losers who look at me as if I'm insane
when I tell them that even if they depart one dollar
ahead—that is a triumph. *One dollar!* A victory.

Winning is important. Dame Fortune will take care
of the numbers. Sometimes you'll streak lucky and
come away with much more than you sought. Other
times the amount will seem disappointing—though it
will look better the next day.

This is what happens when discipline erodes. I consider it Danger Time.

I took a 10 A.M. TWA flight from New York. I
checked into the Riviera at 1 P.M. At about 10 P.M. I
checked out. I was $24,860 ahead for a nine-hour visit.

Then I did that dumb thing which I am susceptible to
when I'm tired. I had a half-hour to spare. I walked to
baccarat, stood there and called large bets. I lost. My
winning total shrank.

Time had run out if I was to make my flight. I had
twelve white chips ($6,000) in my hand. The cashier's
cage is a few yards away from the baccarat table. But I
was just too exhausted to care. My self-discipline was
gone. I couldn't wait to lose.

I hurried to my car.

After the plane took off, I took a count and made a
final report into my Norelco. I was still $3,457 ahead.*
I knew that I could hate myself for my stupidity in losing back so much because I so clearly violated my own
rules. But I knew, too, that I would feel better about
$3,457 the next day.

I was, after all, a winner.

*This was my April 7, 1977, trip. See the list of ten in the
introduction to this book.

I'm an ice cream freak. You can buy a lot of ice cream cones for $3,457.

What happens from gaming session to gaming session is important but not critical. What really counts is HOW YOU LEAVE.

THE FINAL NUMBER. THE BOTTOM LINE.

Temporary losses don't matter if you're self-disciplined. For self-discipline will overcome even those disadvantageous odds! One of my personal rules is never to gamble on the last day in the casino where you have credit. And not to gamble at all in the three hours before you leave. This time, time was too short. But I had violated the rule in spirit—and paid a high toll for doing so.

Let me tell you how my Norelco cassette played an important role on another visit.

That trip even began with a difference. During my first hour at the baccarat table, the fellow to my right held the shoe for nineteen passes. I understand this is close to the house record of twenty-one straight Bank wins.

I was betting with him all the way—though unbelieving most of the way. Then I got lucky with dice. On to another hotel and more winnings.

When I counted up I was just under $50,000 ahead.

I had been in town less than four hours.

Jump on a plane and get out? Ah, but I was in a bind. A lady friend was joining me in two days. I was committed to stay in Las Vegas for four days.

Do you see immediately how this violated my own canon of behavior? And why I say: If you're serious about winning, go alone.

I phoned my son Rory, who was playing jazz guitar in Boulder, Colorado. He agreed to fly to visit with me for a few hours the next day.

By the time he arrived, I was down to $30,000 ahead.

My son disapproves of my gambling. He feels that gamblers are fools—a sentiment in which I concur. He sees neither fun nor excitement in it. It bores him.

So it was that while he was with me I didn't gamble.

He left. My lady arrived. I won some, and I lost some. But I was locked into casino roving and, thus, doing far too much playing.

After a time, Lady Luck turned her sour face to me. I ignored my own rules. I lost. From place to place, percentage chopped away at me.

Late that night—or, rather, at 2 A.M.—we returned to the room and had begun to undress when I handed my lady friend a thick pack of money. "Go downstairs and walk straight to the baccarat table and put this on Player," I told her.

She did. The bet won. The uncounted money stack I gave her consisted of thirty $100 bills, so she returned to the room with $6,000.

"I just wanted to go to sleep after a winning wager," I explained.

But I had the Las Vegas disease of overstimulation. I'd been in town too long. At 6 A.M. I was downstairs again and quickly lost the last of my ready cash.

Tapped out. Or, as the late Toots Shor used to say, "Tapioca."

I came back to the suite. I sat in the living room and relayed the latest bad turn into the cassette. Then, out of curiosity, I played the whole thing back.

Early on, I had talked into it about a fellow who had lost $100,000 cash at baccarat. He asked for $2,000 "get-out-of-town" money: and was given it.*

*This is also known as "broke money" and though you, like myself, may never avail yourself of it, you should know about it. If you gamble a large amount of money and go broke in a casino, you can always ask for—and get—cash enough to remove you from the scene of your disaster.

"Broke money" is not a small incidental in casino overhead. Some years ago, Jack Binion of the Horseshoe Club reported that he was giving away $12,000 a month in "broke money."

But instead of getting out of town, he sat down at the table and began to play again. When he left Las Vegas, he had won back the $100,000 and another $100,000.

A pit boss had told me the story concluding with the moral, which in his words was that "A man isn't dead until his ass is cold."

A MAN ISN'T DEAD UNTIL HIS ASS IS COLD!

I thought it an amusing enough story when I heard it to relate it into the cassette recorder. But that was when things were amusing because I was ahead $50,000.

Now I was out of cash and down $42,000. I had come to town to win. I had won nearly $50,000, and then, like a jerk, I had thrown my rules to the wind and turned my big win into a depressing loss.

A MAN ISN'T DEAD UNTIL HIS ASS IS COLD. I thought about it. I certainly seemed "dead"—and yet I felt full of positive energy.

I knew how to tap another $20,000 worth of playing money. I did.

But first I searched my own true feelings. I decided the urge to play some more was not the loser's usual self-destructive drive. I did not intend to lose.

Downstairs I went. I had only a few hours before a scheduled departure to Los Angeles.

By flight time I had won back the $42,000, and then some.

It was my fifth trip. Plus $7,412.

Not the fifty grand I could have left with. But *a winner*.

A MAN ISN'T DEAD UNTIL HIS ASS IS COLD.

WHAT COUNTS IS THE FINAL COUNT—THE MONEY IN YOUR POCKET WHEN YOU BOARD THE PLANE TO LEAVE TOWN.

19

The fastest game in town

Baccarat and craps. Craps and baccarat. I like 'em both
for the money I can take from them. In the early part of
my ten winning visits, I took most of the winnings from
dice tables. During the later visits, it was mostly baccarat.

Baccarat can be fast and it can be rough, so when I
just wet my feet I had determined to stay with dice.

"Be strong," I told myself. "Put your blinders on and
walk past all baccarat tables without placing a wager."

I was a hero to myself. I did.

But then came a time when dice were sour and I
didn't have the feeling they were about to change for
me. I needed to recoup a fair number of dollars.

Baccarat. I would win it there.

I did.

Black-tie baccarat, Las Vegas style, was brought to
Vegas from Havana by the late Francis "Tommy" Renzoni.

The Vegas version of the "big nine" game is "automated" in that there are no decisions to make with regard to the cards.

In Chemin de Fer, if a player has a total of five, he must decide whether or not to ask for a third card. The draw is optional. And the player's job is to fool the person banking the game. In Vegas, the player *must* draw a card.

In Chemin de Fer, the gamble is limited by the amount the bank is willing to lose. In Vegas baccarat you can play against the casino's entire bankroll.

Moreover, the player can decide to play Bank or Player and to switch sides from hand to hand. He is thus given a chance to outguess the deck.

There is nothing mysterious about baccarat. It is a game that anyone can play. You have only two decisions to make.

1. How much will you bet?
2. Which side will you bet on?

You place your money on either Bank or Player and wait. Everything that happens thereafter is quite automatic, with the dealers directing, according to rules, whether or not bank and/or player receive a third card after each are dealt two.

First, the amount you can bet. In some casinos the minimum is as low as $5. In most Strip hotels the minimum is $20. The maximum in some places is $2,000, and in others, $4,000.

Caesars Palace, which runs as many as three action-packed tables simultaneously, allows a betting range of $20 to $4,000. Ditto the Dunes.

At this writing there are other casinos which allow $4,000, but they're running scared and allow $4,000 bets only if your smallest bet is $500. I happen to think this is nonsense and you should play where you can bet up to $4,000 without *any* minimum bet requirement.

Be selective. For example, the Aladdin has this restrictive rule. But it also has the best free odds schedule at the dice table. Caesars Palace has the best baccarat range, but it allows only single odds at dice. So play dice at the Aladdin and baccarat at Caesars Palace or the Dunes.

(And again, keep in mind that rules change all the time so that by the time you're reading this, they may have changed again. It doesn't cost a thimbleful of mule piss to ask questions before you play.)

Baccarat is a guessing game. It's a heads-or-tails affair. Because of the way rules are structured, Bank has a slight edge and will usually (but not always) win a few more hands in a shoe than Player will win.

It is startling to survey the ignorance about the game which exists even in seasoned gamblers. For example, I know a man who flies to Las Vegas every Saturday and returns to New York every Monday.

The hotel he stays at keeps a suite for him at all times. It's called The Diplomat Suite. We'll call him Mr. Chong because that isn't his name.

At any rate, he's a big-money craps player. Even at grind hotels like the MGM Grand, he plays $4,000 and $8,000 at the dice table by special arrangement.

He plays at five casinos. At each, he has $100,000 credit. He settles for cash before he leaves town.

You can imagine how they love him!

He thinks he has a great deal on accommodations. His hotel gives him extra security protection. And his arrangement with all five hotels is that if he is a big loser, they allow him the cost of two first class, round-trip tickets to the Philippines!*

That's about $4,200 for the pair.

If he's a small loser, $10,000 or less, he doesn't bother about the tickets. If he is a large loser, he asks for and gets that cash refund. If he loses big in four

---

*He owns a large sugar business of some kind in the Philippines—though he travels there only twice a year. Charging the casino for that long distance trip is the little game he plays with their knowledge and consent.

casinos, he gets the cash price ($4,200) for two tickets from each of the four casinos!

Needless to say, over any period of time he loses hundreds of thousands of dollars. Needless to say, he can afford it.

In conversation with him I mentioned that I had begun to like baccarat even more than dice. Oh, no, he explained, because *they take 5% at baccarat!*

If even a big-money player like Mr. Chong is that ignorant, it is no wonder that baccarat hasn't outdistanced the other casino games in popularity. It should. I happen to believe it gives you the best chance—if you're willing to win and walk.

As to the 5%, this is the explanation. The casino gives Player even odds. If you bet $100 on Player and win, you are paid $100.

Since the rules of the game favor the Bank side, the casino pays off 95¢ against your dollar for winning bets on the Bank side. But it would take forever to pay people 95¢ for each dollar wagered. So what they do is to pay you even money—$100 for your $100 bet—and mark up $5 against your seat (which even they mistakenly call "commission").

It isn't "commission." They pay you $1 but only owe you 95¢. The 5¢ they charge against you is the change you owe them. Period.

What's so great about baccarat?

For one thing, the odds against you are even smaller than those against Do and Don't line bets at craps.

The odds against Player bets are 1.35% and the odds against Bank bets are even smaller: approximately 1.20%.

For another thing, look at the range of the wagers you can make. In no other casino game can you put down $4,000 on either side and in less time than it takes to read this, win or lose. On Players side you're paid $4,000. On Bank side you're paid $4,000 but owe $200 change. (All clear?)

In no other game can you bet comparatively small amounts—guess wrong and lose ten bets in a row—and then make one big one and win back all your losses, and then some.

It's quick and it's clean.

Results can run in streaks. This can break the novice. He observes that the Bank has won four or five times and is convinced that it's time for Player to win. But Bank can win another four or five times. Or the pattern might run Bank, Player, Bank, Player, Bank, Bank, Player, Player.

Baccarat obviously requires a certain amount of luck and perhaps a certain unconscious sense of the rhythm of the cards. People who believe they have systems or try to count against a shoe containing eight (or at some casinos, nine) decks of cards are destined to be losers.

The action and suspense are the greatest.

Baccarat has style. Note the atmosphere with the dealers in formal attire. It is the casino's "class game." It has status.

It can also make a quick fortune for the casino.

Last year the Sands had a happy experience. Twelve men and women flew to Las Vegas from Japan. They occupied all the seats. They spoke Japanese and they talked fluently to each other.

The Sands limit was $2,000. But now twelve players each bet $2,000 so that they were, in fact, betting $24,000 per hand.

They had a system. Obviously someone had worked out a way to destroy the casinos. They did all kinds of figuring with felt-tipped pens on rectangle-shaped pads, and the chatter never ceased.

When they quit fourteen hours after they'd begun, the English speaking croupiers hadn't understood one word that had been spoken. The supervisors understood only one thing: the group had lost $1,250,000, almost to the penny.

The Sands quickly sought and found a Japanese-speaking dealer. They needn't have bothered. The group hasn't returned.

Recently, after being trimmed at the Sands by my favorite barber, Tony Pepe, I passed that same baccarat table. Someone I knew walked up and called a $2,000 bet on Player.

He won.

He stood there and called the same bet. He won again.

He picked up his $4,000 in chips and the two of us were about to head to the cashier on the other side of the room, when a man who had just sat down and lost his first bet on Bank complained: "I picked a good time to sit down!"

The $4,000 winner called another $2,000 bet on Player. He won again. He'd won $6,000 in less than five minutes.

"Why did you make that third bet when you were just about to walk away?" I asked him.

"Lyle, old buddy," he said, "I was thrilled silly with that $4,000 win. But then I heard that fellow, and he was an echo of what I would say when, for instance, I'd sit at a blackjack table and on the first deal to me the dealer would turn over his blackjack. I don't recall ever starting that way and then turning into an immediate winner. So I had a hunch this fellow was going to lose his second bet, too. It was a dumb hunch but it was the right one!"

Never argue with success.

20

To tip or not to tip

I have a certain contempt for money. Sure, I've been uncomfortable without it for it is a short-cut to pleasure and comfort. But money itself has never been my primary goal: neither accumulating it nor accumulating the things it buys. I'm not a collector and there are few material possessions that I could not do without.

All of this by way of explaining that my attitudes need not be your attitudes on tips and tipping.

There is no reason to tip dealers and no need to tip dealers.

That being said, let me add that I'm one of the most generous tippers I know. I tip early and sometimes I tip often. I do it by making two-way hard-way bets for the dealers at the dice table and two-way $100 bets at baccarat. (Two-ways at baccarat means that if the wager is won and becomes $200 it will be divided between the dealers and the starters or shills.)

I never tip when I feel there is any pressure on me to tip. If a stickman or croupier tries to promote me with the sometimes heard, "Why not make a little bet for the boys?" there is no way I tip.

My tipping is instinctive and voluntary.

Tipping can't change the face of a single card or the turn of a single die. It cuts into your winnings.

Why do it then?

You don't have to.

Why do I do it? Because usually I like dealers and starters and I enjoy having them share my good luck when I have it. I want to feel a positive atmosphere at the tables. I want them to be rooting for me, too. (And they do.)

I'm known widely enough so that when I lose the dealers know they're losing too.

My tips have come to as much as $2,000 to $3,000 on a big winning trip.

Although tipping was once permitted in British casinos, it is now strictly prohibited. The theory is that tipping the dealers gives them a vested interest in the outcome of the play and might ultimately lead to collusion between dealers and players.

Nobody has offered any collusion to me but it isn't a bad feeling to know that seven or eight people at a table genuinely want me to win.

Once, many years ago at the Sands, Tommy Renzoni was about to close the game. Baccarat wasn't a twenty-four-hour proposition in those days.

I was doing good. "How about one more shoe, Tommy?"

Tommy turned to his crew. "Do you want to deal one more shoe for Lyle?"

The dealers were exhausted. A youngster named Patrick was having difficulty keeping his eyes open. But they all agreed and they were nice about it.

Patrick was on his relief break and I was doing well with the shoe when suddenly I announced: "A thousand dollar bet for the dealers on Players."

I held the shoe. After a stunned silence, someone said, "You mean on Bank."

"No. I mean on Player."

I dealt Player a total of 2. I dealt Bank a total of 1. The third card for each of them was a 9.

Player had a final total of 1, beating Bank, which had broken to 0.

It was at this moment that Patrick returned to the table. He needed toothpicks to hold his eyelids apart. One of the dealers beckoned to him and whispered in his ear: *"Stuart just made a thousand dollar bet for us and it won!"*

Patrick woke up like a shot. The smile on his face was almost worth the $2,000.

Today, he's a dealer at the Dunes. When I first played there in 1977, no more than a few minutes had passed when he said, "Do you remember that night—"

"I was just thinking about it," I said.

Patrick broke into another broad smile.

I don't happen to smoke. I happen to think cigarette smokers are natural-born losers. If you're a cigarette smoker, you're going to disagree.

But don't disagree with me about alcohol. It's free and plentiful in every casino. And it's for all the players at all the tables, except you.

You want to have a clear mind.

Contrary to the b.s. about a drink or two "clearing your head" or "relaxing you" there is no way that alcohol will do anything except dull your reflexes, your intuition, your true feelings, and your discipline.

Drinking while gambling will not only help you to lose but it will make the loss seem less painful.*

*The Commission on the Review of the National Policy Toward Gambling found a relationship between gambling and alcohol consumption. "People who bet," said the report, "say they consume alcohol on four times as many days as people

Drink all the booze you want to drink. At home. At the office. At your local pub.

Do not drink while you gamble.

End of sermon.

who don't bet at all. As the dollar volume of betting increases, so does alcohol consumption. . . . It is impossible to state whether gambling activities increase alcohol consumption or vice versa but the relationship is strong."

21

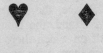

More about the game of baccarat

When I play baccarat, I try to limit myself to two complete shoes. I don't like to begin in the middle of a shoe. I like to keep score.

Years ago in Europe, and particularly at the casinos of Wiesbaden (the only major casino that ever tried to cheat me!) and Bad Homburg, I used to look with some disdain at those people at roulette tables who compulsively kept records of every turn of the wheel. Old-time faro players kept scorecards with buttons, but that suicidal game is almost obsolete today.

Today, I rarely play baccarat without keeping score.

The scorecard (called *Table de Banque* by dealers who can't speak any other word of French) talks to me. It tells me things I need to know. It alerts me to trends and possibilities.

Play two full shoes and then take a walk. Only if you are iron-disciplined about yourself and have won a lot of money and have carefully segregated a small amount which if you lose you'll walk—should you remain.

Over and over and over again I have watched winners turn to losers by sitting too long.

Okay, you're sitting down. You've begun to play the guessing game. I will now share with you the complete results (except for ties) of 95 full shoes that I've played at various times on my ten winning trips. These were played at Caesars Palace, the Riviera, the Sands, the Aladdin, the MGM Grand, the Dunes and the Hilton.

Total hands dealt on which there were decisions (in other words in which there were no ties) were 6,842.

3,539 hands were won by the Bank side.

3,303 hands were won by the Player side.

If you had bet $100 on each hand and won every Bank hand, you'd have been paid a net of $336,205. If you had won every Player hand you'd have been paid $330,300. You can see the slim margin that favors Bank bettors even at 95¢ to $1 odds.

Following are the sequences in the 95 full shoes I played.

What is the value of record-keeping?

For one thing, if you look at column three you'll see that a 2-time sequence will occur a little less than half as many times as a one-time sequence. A 3-timer half as many as a two. A 4-timer half as many as a three. A 5-time sequence half as many times as a four.

"So what?" you say. "That's after the fact. How can that help me?"

Let me tell you how it has occasionally helped me.

I've been halfway through a shoe and not doing particularly well. I knew that I had to chance some large bets and to win most of them if I were to leave the table a winner. The scorecard talked to me. It confirmed to me that the shoe was chopping like crazy. But I noticed that single banks had come up eleven times and a double bank had come up only twice.

Sequences:	Bank	Player	Total	Total Hands*
1 time	847	926	1773	1773
2 times	413	406	819	1638
3 times	208	200	408	1224
4 times	115	100	215	860
5 times	66	41	107	535
6 times	38	28	66	396
7 times	7	8	15	105
8 times	7	8	15	120
9 times	5	3	8	72
10 times	2	1	3	30
11 times	1	1	2	22
12 times	2	2	4	48
19 times	1	—	1	19
	1712	1724	3436	6842

*Ties also came up a total of 698 times.

Now, in all of my tedious card analysis, I didn't recall a single shoe score in which Bank didn't average almost half as many 2's as 1's. Remembering that the improbable does happen, I knew it was possible. But my experience went against it.

So what did I do?

I sat out hands. Until Bank won. Then I placed a large bet on Bank.

I made this bet four times and won three. At $2,000 a crack I was $4,000 ahead for my scorecard-reading. More, since I knew that Bank was due for sequences of 2 (and no more) immediately after winning on that second Bank win, I made a smaller bet on Player. Again I won three out of four.

It pays to know what's happening. In this case it paid me a profit of $4,600 after so-called commissions on the $4,000.

I have stressed how costly ignorance can be.

In September, 1977, I sat at a baccarat table for a short time and lost money. I left. But not before I had observed a plainly dressed man who was betting $6,000 on Bank. The house limit at that casino was $4,000. To qualify for the higher limit, one needed a solid $100,000 or better line of credit.

The fellow certainly had it. He was playing from a high stack of yellow ($1,000) chips.

It was 2 A.M. I went upstairs to sleep.

In the morning, feeling refreshed and good, I returned to the table. It was 8:30 A.M. He was still there. He was joined by a slighter fellow who, I was told, was his brother.

I had assumed the two were Spanish. They were Arabs.

The brother was betting $4,000 a card. He also was betting exclusively on the Bank side.

Every hand!

It isn't unusual for a baccarat game to go at a pace of two hands a minute. Half-hour for a shoe. Seventy to seventy-five decisions.

The brothers were gambling $720,000 every half-hour. And paying the casino its percentage of about $18,00 an hour. There was *no way* they could win betting every single hand on Bank.

Crazy? In Monte Carlo they talk about a Russian count who bet huge amounts on *every* number for each roll of the roulette wheel. He always had the winning number.

So here were two Arab brothers who didn't really understand the primary rules of what they were doing.

Did I tip them off? What? With the price of gasoline where it is? Not even in jest!

22

Sharing my experience

Here are some observations I can make after many years of playing the game.

1. "Starters" or shills are nice people. They don't affect your chances either way.

2. Once the cards are in the shoe, the die is cast (to use an old cliché from "Bomba the Jungle Boy"). What happens now depends on which side you bet and how much you bet.

3. If you are guessing wrong, sit it out for a while. Sit, watch and don't bet.

4. If you start with a certain stake and you've lost a part of it and don't feel good at all about the game, you are under no contract to remain. Leave at any time.

That's one thing in your favor about casinos. They're always there for you to take a shot at their money but they can't take a shot at yours except when you decide to allow it.

Reminder: If three Player or Bank wins come up in a row, your proper move is either to bet on a fourth in the sequence or not to bet at all.

Just as a monkey could throw the dice, a barking seal could be trained to deal a baccarat shoe. Nevertheless, we're all human and get strong feelings about other people. If we don't care for someone's look or style, we tend to bet against them. If we like 'em, we sometimes bet with 'em even against our own strong instincts!

When the shoe is passed to you and Player has won the previous three hands, you *must* bet Player. You'll win as often as you lose. The fact that you're holding the shoe doesn't change the face of a single card in it. (God has not taken time out from counting the proceeds in the big collection plate in the sky to look down and turn that queen of spades into a nine of clubs because you once won brownie points as a Boy Scout.)

So, even though it "goes against your grain"—bet Player. It can be a small bet. If you lose, you'll still have the shoe and now you can bet Bank.

If it is psychologically impossible for you to bet against yourself while you're dealing, then simply pass the shoe this time.

Keeping in mind that the improbable happens and that gaming results are often a paradox, what do you do if you know that an average shoe ends with thirty-four Bank wins and thirty-one Player wins, and now the shoe has shown forty-five Player wins and there are about four hands left?

I know clever fellows who would respond: "I'd bet heavily on Bank catching up."

It could. And then again maybe it won't.

I go with the trend. If Player has come up 45, it could come up 5 more.

In this tome I didn't burden you with rules of craps. I assume that you know them—or can pick them up with ease elsewhere. But for the Mr. Chongs among you, let me say of baccarat that the game is so simple as to seem silly. Perhaps it is its stark simplicity that has kept it going for some five hundred years.

It's a game of nines. You want the side you bet on to have a total of 9—or as close to it as possible. Eight is better than seven; seven better than six, etc.

The person holding the shoe deals two cards to the Player and two to himself. They're dealt face down but it wouldn't affect results—only suspense—if they were dealt face up.

When either hand has a 2-card total of 8 or 9 (called naturals), the hand is over—no one draws a third card. 9 beats 8 and ties stand off.

The Player is first to act and will always draw a third card having a hand total of 0, 1, 2, 3, 4, or 5. With 6 or 7 the Player stands.

When the Player draws or stays, the Bank automatically draws to 0, 1 and 2. When the Player stands with a total of 6 or 7, the Bank draws having 0, 1, 2, 3, 4, 5, stands having 6 or 7.

With a count of 3, 4, 5, 6, whether the Bank draws a third card or stands is determined by the face value of the third card the Player draws.

If the Bank has a count of 3, he draws a third card only when dealing 1, 2, 3, 4, 5, 6, 7, 9, 10 as the Player third card. He does not draw when dealing an 8.

If the Bank has a count of 4, he draws a third card only when dealing a 2, 3, 4, 5, 6, 7 as the Player third card. He does not draw when dealing a 1, 8, 9, 10.

If the Bank has a count of 5, he draws when dealing a 4, 5, 6, 7 as the Player third card. He does not draw when dealing a 1, 2, 3, 8, 9, 10.

And when the Bank has a count of 6, he draws only when dealing a 6 or 7 as the Player third card. He does not draw when dealing any other card. The Bank always stands having 7.

Pictures and tens count as zero. Since the goal is 9, a total of 10 counts for zero. Thus 6 and 5 add up to 1. 3 and 9 add up to 2.

Every casino has, free for the asking, a card that explains the rules.

But you don't have to know the rules!

The table has three dealers. Two are seated and take care of paying and collecting money, paying off bets, making change and changing cash to chips. The third, the croupier, stands and directs the player dealing from the shoe. He calls for the initial cards. Then he announces the totals for each side. He requests a further card for either or both sides if the rules call for it. He announces the winner.

The cards lie there, face up, until all wagers are settled.

Baccarat gives the Las Vegas Strip casinos about 12% of their profits. These from a comparatively few players.

Not bad?

I don't know any other casino game that can so frighten gambling bosses. The game can win big money but it can also lose it.

The Aladdin once lost a quarter of a million dollars to three winners in three days, and closed the game for three months.

The Riviera recently installed a larger shoe and deals sixteen instead of eight decks.* It also cut its maximum

---

*One reason for this may be that casinos know that when a shoe is ended, players tend to leave. That's "get away" time. Commissions are settled and people get up to stretch, go to the john, etc. The notion that by doubling the decks you'll keep 'em longer may seem sound, but I doubt that it is. People need an occasional rest break. The Union Plaza once had the longest shoe in the world: 144 decks. It was amusing to watch, but few took it seriously and the shoe was removed.

to $2,000. It is running scared. To bet $4,000, you have to have $25,000 cash on deposit in its cage. (The Riviera, incidentally, is the only super casino in which I've ever seen a top executive grab dice from the table and remove them from play in the middle of a hand. Not because there was anything wrong with the dice, but rather because the young lady throwing them was doing exceedingly well and costing the house some money.) At the Riviera, they hate you to win.

Other casinos are being forced to move in the direction of $4,000 maximums. But they cling to the $5 to $2,000 (or $20 to $2,000) and $500 to $4,000.

In short, if you want to bet up to $4,000 your minimum bet must always be $500.

The theory seems to be that this way the progressive bettor will be stopped.

I've had some friendly arguments with casino bosses at the Sands about this. I pointed out that $20 to $2,000 allows for a sequence of 7 wagers: $20, $40, $80, $160, $320, $640, $1,280. $500 to $4,000 allows for only four progressive bets: $500, $1,000, $2,000, $4,000.

With the smaller limit, the player would be risking $2,540 in seven bets to win a big $20. If, for example, he played every bank hand listed on my total chart of 6,842 hands (page 125), he would win $33,740 and lose almost twice that. For sequences of 7, 8, 9 and 10 do occur, though not often.

The further explanation is that the people in charge of the Sands don't want a small player to get into the game with a little money and then have a shot at their bankroll in a big way if he gets lucky.

I argued that if a man works his stake up to $4,000—why not allow him to bet the $4,000? It's the same bet, with the same odds against, that a new a person coming into a game would have if he sat down and made a $4,000 first bet.

The reasoning? The house didn't want someone with

their money to hurt them. *Their* money! The casino boss I discussed this with continued to insist that if a man came into a game with $300 and soon had $3,300, the $3,000 was *their* (the casino's) money!

It's just as dumb on the other side. How often have you heard a player say, "It's okay, I'm using *their* money."

When you win, it is no longer *their* money. It's your money. And when you lose it's no longer *your* money, it's *theirs!*

All clear?

Tommy Renzoni (who brought baccarat to Las Vegas) used to insist to me that when someone he knew came in and sat at the table, he could tell after just a few hands whether that person would be a winner or loser for the session.

It didn't matter, insisted Tommy, whether the player won or lost those first few bets. It was just something about him. Attitude, maybe. Tommy and I once sat in Gramercy Park while he talked about his dream. He wanted to open a really classy baccarat casino. Nothing but baccarat. $100 minimum bets.

He wanted the place open only from maybe 9 P.M. until 3 A.M.

"But Tommy," I said, "everybody else is open twenty-four hours a day."

He looked at me with his soft wide eyes.

"Lyle," he said, "I've been in the gambling business all of my life. Nobody is ever going to play with my money while I'm sleeping!"

Although Tommy supervised the game at the Sands and saw fortunes lost, he was himself a prisoner of the gaming fever. He would gather a stake of $30,000 and hurry over to Caesars Palace—where he generally lost.

Once he won $42,000 and suffered a slight heart attack. He was rushed to the hospital. The next evening he got up from his bed, dressed himself, signed himself out of the hospital in front of two bewildered nurses and an intern, and taxied to Caesars Palace, where he quickly dropped the $42,000.

There are few baccarat games today which don't have one or more of "Tommy's boys"—the crew that worked with him in the original Sands game.

Tommy's wife died of cancer. Months later he visited a friend at the Tropicana and complained about how he couldn't shake the depression he felt about his wife's death.

Then he went outside and walked in front of a speeding car. He was killed instantly.

Frank Sinatra may be a hero to Spiro Agnew but he was no hero to baccarat dealers. He was noisy and rude. He made demands that he knew couldn't be met. He insulted casino employees.

He had an $8,000-a-hand limit but kept insisting that he wanted $16,000. He would often hold up the game, hand after hand, insisting on the $16,000.

Instructions were very firm. Sinatra was not to be dealt cards unless he committed himself.

"Mr. Sinatra, are you shilling or going for the money?"

He balked at answering. Too often he had played and then gotten up and said he was "only fooling" or "just being a shill for you"—and refused to make good his losses.

No commitment, no cards.

Over the course of a few weeks, Sinatra and Beverly Hills real estate broker Danny Schwartz had won nearly a million dollars from Caesars Palace. They'd collected every penny.

Now, Sinatra, doing a solo, was losing it back rapidly. But instead of cash he was papering the cage with markers.

On the night of drama, instructions were to cut off his credit when he owed $400,000. He still had a handful of white ($500 chips) with him but kept insisting on another $25,000.

The croupier called the casino manager, Sandy Waterman. Sandy, usually cool and wise, should have sent security men to the troubled baccarat pit. Instead, he hurried over himself.

"Frank," he explained, "you owe us four hundred big ones. If you want more you've got to pay off something. The boys want their money."

Sinatra stood up. He flung his white chips into Sandy Waterman's face, at the same time smacking him on the forehead with the palm of his hand.

Waterman turned and ran to his room. Within minutes he returned with a loaded gun in his hand. He pointed it at the singer.

"Listen you! If you ever lay a hand on me again I'll put a bullet through your head!" Sanford Waterman had lost his cool.

Sinatra hadn't lost his. "Aw, come on," he said with a disparaging gesture, "that gun stuff went out with Humphrey Bogart!"

Disconcerted by Sinatra's nonchalant response, Waterman's arm lowered just enough for one of Sinatra's gofers to strike it. The gun fell to the floor. Waterman knew he was in trouble. He turned and ran to the cage, with Sinatra and his wolf pack in hot pursuit.

Sinatra's left arm was in a sling, the result of some surgery on his veins.

The cashier cage door opened. Waterman tried to close it behind him but Sinatra clung to it. The door smashed back against his bad arm. Blood spurted upward. Everyone stood appalled. The drama was over as Sinatra hurried to his third floor suite and a gofer went for the house doctor.

The baccarat scene is never dull.

Keeping the baccarat scoreboard

Except for the Hilton, every major Strip casino will furnish you with scorecards for your baccarat game. The Hilton will give you a blank pad.

The cards all resemble the one on the next page.

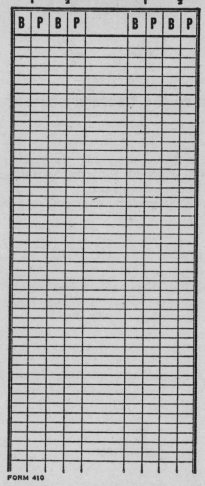

Many players who keep score do it with X's this way:

STARDUST
BACCARAT GAME

B	P	P	B	P		B	P	B	P
	X								
X									
X	X								
X									
X	X								
X									
X	X								
X									
X									
X									

I require more information than that. So, I arrive with both red and black Pentel pens. I number the decisions and I use black for a lost bet, red for a winning bet. (Winning bets are indicated with check marks.) Black, circled, indicates a hand in which I didn't bet.

Ties are indicated by a flat line.*

On page 138 is the reproduction of the results of an actual shoe. I have picked a winning card with a not untypical run of decisions.

Note that I played only 66 of the 77 hands. Note, too, that I won 33 of the 66—or exactly half. Yet when the shoe ended I was $11,600 ahead on this one.

---

*Ties pay 8 to 1. They are similar to proposition bets at craps. The percentage is too heavy against you.

BACCARAT GAME

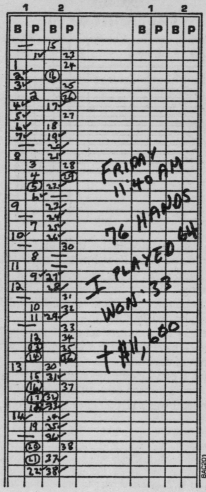

BAC201

On June 28, 1977, I made my fourteenth 1977 journey to Las Vegas. I went directly from the airport to the MGM Grand Hotel. The house rule was that even though there were nothing but starters (shills) at the table, the dealers weren't allowed to mix a new shoe until the old one was dealt out.

I played some dice for small stakes, winning about $1,800.

I returned to the baccarat table. The shoe appeared to have another ten minutes to go, but finally, in defeat, the pit boss directed the dealers to stop the charade and make a new shoe.

I played two complete shoes. I had arrived at the airport at 11:15 A.M., and when the second shoe ended, it was 1:30 P.M. I was studying my wristwatch. I had plenty of time to catch TWA's flight 148 back to New York.

Terrific!

I counted my money. Including the dice win I was $23,250 ahead.

Then there occurred one of those freak encounters—the kind that only seem to happen to gamblers. A stranger sat down next to me while the dealers were shuffling the cards for a new shoe that I didn't intend to play.

"Damn!" he exclaimed.

Quite naturally I asked, "What's the matter?"

"Oh, hell! I'm supposed to take a 2:30 plane to New York and it's been delayed two hours."

I knew he was talking about TWA—the "on time" airline. I knew also and straight away that I wasn't going to permit this information to keep me at the table. In all of Las Vegas at all of the baccarat tables this fellow had to sit next to and share his troubles with me!

Had he not sat down, I would have driven to the airport, turned in my Hertz car, and happily sat in the lounge reading magazines, newspapers and books to pass the two hours.

I went to a public phone. Yes, said the girl from TWA, #148 was delayed. It wouldn't depart until 4:30.

I reserved a First Class seat. (On this one-stop trip I was picking up my own airfare and it had been deducted from winnings.)

I hurried out of the casino to the shopping arcade. I had my photograph taken with "Leo, the MGM lion" for $15.

Then I got into my rented automobile and sped downtown to one of the small joints that advertise payoffs of 98% on slots. It took me fifteen minutes to get rid of $2 worth of nickels and ten minutes to get rid of $20 in Eisenhower dollars. I was time-passing, euphoric and bored.

I played some dice. The house had a $100 limit including odds. I played blackjack. $50 limit. Suddenly, without seeming to, I had pissed away $740.

I was annoyed with myself. I got in the car again and started for the airport. I struggled against the urge to stop off at a "regular" casino and win it back.

I lost the struggle and pulled into the Stardust.

They were mixing a new shoe. It was afternoon and I was the only real player. I bet $800 on the first deal. I won.

I won the next three bets.

I lost 9 of the next 11. When I stood up I had lost all the cash in my pocket.

Do not despair, dear reader—all the cash *wasn't* all the money I had won.

This time I controlled the urge to pull into Caesars Palace and win back my new larger loss.

At the airport I counted my currency. Deducting all expenses, I was still $14,250 ahead.

Which brings us to the subject of money management, except that first I want to show you the two MGM cards. Note that on the two cards combined there were 138 hands dealt not counting 17 ties.

Of these I played 114. Of these I won 66.

That's better than half. However, I must point out that often I win fewer than half the hands I bet and still walk away a big money winner.

There isn't a lot of rhyme or reason to the play you see here except that you should observe that at no time did I buck a trend of three or more. On the contrary, note on the second card, I bet and lost three times in a row against Player. My choice then was either to bet Player or not to bet at all.

I switched to Player and won the next six hands.

What follows is my money strategy at baccarat.

I'll talk in terms of my own numbers and you can translate these down (or up) into your own money amounts.

I'll bet $4,000. If I win, I take the winnings and reduce my wager to $2,000. Now, win or lose I'm $2,000 ahead.

If I win the second time, I play for $2,500. Then $3,000. Then $3.500.

With five successive winning bets I have won $15,000 on Player. On Bank it is $15,000 less the "commission" of $750, or a net profit of $14,250.

Sequences of 5 don't come up that often. (Look back at my 95 game record.) Nevertheless, they do come up.

At this point I often drop down to $2,000 again. Or $1,000. I'm not greedy. I'm willing to have the stake build up again if I'm into one of those 7 or 8 or 10 sequences!

Okay. Let's imagine I'm playing Bank. If I lose the first bet, I lost $4,000.

If I win one but lose the second, I'm ahead a net of $1,800.

If I win two bets but lose the third bet, I'm ahead $3,200.

If I win three bets but lose the fourth bet, I'm ahead $5,075.

If I win four bets but lose the fifth bet, I'm ahead $7,425.

MGM GRAND HOTEL BACCARAT GAME
11:30 A.M. 6/28/77 (14TH TRIP)

B	P	B	P		B	P	B	P
	1✓				17			
1					18			
	2✓				19			
2✓						20		
						21		
	✓				20			
	3					22		
3✓						23		
4✓					21			
					22✓			
5✓					23✓			
	✓				24✓			
	4					24		
6						25✓		
⑥					25✓			
	5✓					26		
	6✓					27		
	7				26			
	⑧				27			
	9✓				28			
	10✓					28		
	11✓				29✓			
8						29		
					30✓			
	✓					30		
9✓					31✓			
	12✓				32✓			
	13✓				33✓			
					34✓			
⑩								
	⑭							
⑪				DEALT 64 HANDS				
	15			PLAYED 49				
	16							
⑫	⑰			WON 27				
	⑱			+ $8,400				
13✓								
14✓								
15✓								
16	19							

MGM GRAND HOTEL BACCARAT GAME
12:07   2 6/28/77   (14TH TRIP) 2

B	P	B	P		B	P	B	P

DEALT 74 HANDS
PLAYED 65
WON 39
+ #13,050

If I'm bold and win 5 in a row and stay with $3,500 for the 6th and lose that one, I'm still ahead $10,750. If I win and get off, I'm ahead $17,575.

Should I win that one, it's $4,000 a hand all the way with the clear understanding that the house is going to win the final bet—the one I lose.

Let's try a variation. Instead of an initial wager of $4,000, you bet $1,000. Then $2,000. Then $4,000.

You are really wagering that whichever side you are betting with will win one out of three. In which case you will be $1,000 ahead on the Player's side and $950 on the Bank side—depending on which way you've bet.

You're also risking $7,000 with which to do it.

Ain't nothing certain in life. You can lose $7,000.

Let's break it down further. Let's make an initial bet of $500. Then $1,000. Then $2,000. Then $4,000. You're now betting $7,500 against the other side having a run of four consistent winning hands. You stand to profit $500 on Player, less on Bank.

Now let's extend your chance (and violate my "rule of three") by waiting for either side to win two in a row and then starting to bet the other side. Now you're really wagering that the other side won't win six times in a row.

Sometimes shoe after shoe will be dealt out without either Bank or Player winning six hands in a row.

(I should mention in passing that in the days before scorecards, players were not as conscious of Player-winning runs. Thus, if someone held the shoe for a while, everyone would be aware that Bank made 3 and then 4 and then 5 passes. But when Player won hand after hand and the shoe moved around the table, people were less conscious of the fact that Player had won 6 or 7 in a row.)

No matter how lucky you are and no matter how fortunate your runs or your guesses, you won't be lucky forever. Grab the winnings and run!

24

Managing the money

Money management is your key to making it. There are
multiple points of view on how it should be done. Here
are some tips based on my own experience and on some
of my own disaster visits.

1. If you carry cash, always put most of it into a
    safe deposit box. In most Strip hotels they're
    available (without charge) at the cashier's cage.
    In a few places you'll find them at the hotel's
    reception desk. As you win, return to the box to
    deposit the winnings. Get 'em out of your purse
    and into the strongbox. Go to the box as often as
    you need to for this purpose. Having your money
    in the box is one hedge against letting the gam-
    ing fever get you. Even the inconvenience of re-
    turning to the box for more money should cool
    you off. There are too many times when weari-
    ness or a mixture of emotions will cause you to
    go for all the cash on your person.

2.   Set a firm credit limit with your casino credit manager and tell him flatly and firmly to note on your card that if more credit is extended to you than the maximum you're setting for yourself, you won't pay the overage. They'll hate you it, and they'll hate me for telling you this but the credit manager, as charming as he may be (and many are charmers), is not going to be your best friend. He'll be happy to bury you but it's doubtful if he'd take time to be one of the pallbearers.

There is a ploy in Vegas called "stretch and break." When a credit manager sees that you've put a limit of $5,000 or $10,000 or $20,000 on your credit and knows that you'd probably be good for $30,000 or $40,000 or $50,000, he sometimes feels that his job is to extend your credit. Ask and thou shalt receive.

Greed operates on both sides of the table.

Don't fall into the quagmire of extending your credit. Harold S. Smith, Jr., one-time owner of Harolds Club in Reno, also advised against writing checks. He believed in carrying the cash to play with (even depositing it in the cashier's cage and playing against it to show them you're serious) and if that goes, you go.

I've known people who went to Las Vegas for the sunshine. They didn't plan to gamble. But each morning they had to traverse the casino to reach the newspaper stand. The newspaper cost them an average of $20 a day.

Then there is the classic story about the late great Joe E. Lewis. He was a very funny comedian and a very compulsive gambler.

Joe was dining with a pretty lady. She asked him to get her some cigarettes. He couldn't see a cigarette girl in the restaurant so he left the table and obligingly hurried to the notions counter in the lobby. He returned in a few minutes.

When the meal was over, Lewis noticed that the

young lady was about to leave the open pack of cigarettes on the table.

"Better take them with you, honey, they cost me $32,000."

And it wasn't part of his comedy routine.

It happens that way all the time. A compulsive friend will drop a bankroll between dessert and coffee while supposedly making a phone call or visiting the gent's room.

The late Elvis Presley's very competent manager, Col. Tom Parker, is a born loser. He plays roulette and craps and loves those proposition bets at craps.

I once knew a few turkeys to cost him one hundred thousand dollars. He was on his way to Palm Springs and remarked to the Aladdin's Milton Prell that the turkey he'd eaten the evening before had been particularly tasty.

"Would you like some?" Milton asked. "We've got some freshly roasted."

The Colonel was a person known never to turn down a freebie.

"Sure thing," he replied.

While waiting for the kitchen staff to pack four turkeys, the Colonel went to the dice table and lost the hundred big ones.

His name on credit cards and at the tables was "Mr. Snow." And he was a sucker for the free things in life. He would ask for a free box of cigars after having dropped a quarter of a million dollars—enough to buy his own cigar factory.

Just after Elvis' death they were saying in Las Vegas that the real reason the singer had been working again was to help the Colonel pay off some of his casino markers.

25

Where to play

Casinos have personalities. You will have subjective feelings about various casinos. Some will seem cold and distant. Others warm and friendly.

There are many large casinos on the Las Vegas Strip and obviously you won't be able to play in all of them.

Which one(s) do you choose?

I'm reminded of a funny routine that iconoclastic comedian Lenny Bruce used to perform. He talked about "good rooms for performers."

"They say that the Waldorf-Astoria has a good room. Well, if the Waldorf offered $5,000 a week and the men's room of the YMCA offered $5,010—I'll be at the Y like that! [Snaps his fingers.] *That's* a good room!"

The best Las Vegas hotel and casino? The one with the best food? The best show? The sexiest cocktail waitresses? The pleasantest casino personnel? The best tennis courts and/or golf courses?

Sure. For Samson Sucker and Dolly Dope.

Not for you, pal. You're not there for the niceties. You're there to win money, right? (Try to keep that in mind!)

Therefore, *ipso facto*, the best casino is the casino where you win the most.

Repeat after me: *The best casino is where I win!*

Elementary? Not at all. Years ago when I held the record as the worst poker player in the world, I watched one of the best poker players in action. He was so good that we nicknamed him "the Butcher"—for he carved the rest of us up.

Most of us were at the game for the sociability and the fun. Not the Butcher. He was there for the money. He was pleasant and gracious—but not for one long minute did he forget why he was there. It was pleasure for us, business for him.

Watching him taught me why I could never be a top-notch poker winner. When someone at the table was a large loser, I measured my bets accordingly. I was reluctant to pile woes upon woes.

Not the Butcher. He explained it to me succinctly. "Who are you most likely to take money from? The losers, of course. So you must go after losers with a vengeance."

It all sounds logical. Apply it to casino gambling and the directive would seem apparent, yes? Watch your friends. Again and again they will return to those casinos where they are steady losers—where they're so unlucky that even the postage stamp machine won't pay off for them. Again and again they will try to "win back" from or "best" casinos where they drop their money consistently.

That casino where they won some bucks? Oh, yes, they'll play there occasionally too. But the real challenge is head-on against the place that already has (too much of) "their" money.

It's like the proverbial moth feeding itself into the candle flame.

Control yourself. When you run consistently unlucky at any casino, *accept the fact that the casino hasn't been lucky for you.*

Don't fight it. Simply avoid it. But avoid it like a plague. And if you are tempted to "give it another try" then tell the taxi driver to take you to the airport.

You must be on guard at all times. The moment you lose sight of goals—the moment you take your mind off your purpose—you risk becoming victim of your own human frailty—that self-destructive instinct which lies just beneath the surface in all of us.

Casinos thrive for more reasons than those mathematical percentages against you. They have an additional percentage in the human factor. Don't gift 'em with this one!

26

The gambling evil

A United States Government study made in 1974 showed that 61% of all adult Americans placed a bet that year though only 48% said they placed bets on one of the twelve categories of commercial gambling.

The wagers (bets, not losses) on commericial gaming added up to more than twenty-two *billion* dollars, or an average of almost $150 for every American adult. Setting aside those who don't bet, the average yearly wager was $387 per bettor.

Twenty-two billion looks like this: $22,000,000,000 —and it's almost 2% of the total personal income in America for that year. That's more than American women spent that year on new clothes, or than American families spent on restaurant meals and beverages.

Again: that's the amount wagered and not the amount lost. The take-out rates varied from 18.6% for New York's Off Track Betting to less than 4% for bingo games.

The first people to make serious studies of gaming

were economists and they were confounded by the notion that gambling is a losing proposition and therefore irrational.

This conclusion was challenged by William Vickery in 1945. Vickery said that gaming should be measured not by expected money gains but that the money a gambler doesn't have may seem more valuable to him than what he has. He was supported by Alex Rubner,* who wrote: ". . . gambling can be rational when nonpecuniary pleasure or sensations are desired; gambling as an economic goal is only rational when a person's wish to obtain an otherwise unattainably large lump is very strong. Thus gambling for a poor man may be rational."

Here is what some other "experts" have to say on the subject:

L. Monroe Starkey has reported that gaming is ". . . symptomatic of deeper distresses in our social structure—tedious and purposeless occupations, inequitable distribution of the nation's wealth, cheap and inconsistent law enforcement, the Horatio Alger myth of success by sweat in the face of insurmountable economic and social obstacles, the continued stress on personal initiative to the neglect of community responsibility."

The usual view of gambling is that it is destructive to the individual, undermines the work ethic, and that it removes money from the legitimate marketplace. The research of the 1960s developed some less rigid views. For example, the proposition that people gamble beyond their means was disputed as unproven, and the claim that gambling is detrimental to society was countered by the argument that gambling is an outlet for frustrations, a relief from loneliness, and a leveler of class distinction.

*Source: *The Economics of Gambling* by Alex Rubner published in London, 1966.

Some psychological theorists regard gambling as a normal form of recreation, destructive only to those who become addicted to it or get involved in its criminal aspects. In the case of addiction, they claimed, the proper solution is to cure the addict and not condemn gambling per se.

The person who visits a Nevada hotel and casino for the recreation is easy prey for the casino operator. Everywhere he'll be invited to win automobiles, boats, and huge jackpots.

When a jackpot is hit on a slot machine, bells ring, lights flash and often a change girl announces the news on a loudspeaker.

The prestige-seeking drives of a player are catered to by expensive, ostentatious architecture and decor, and his desire for recreational fun is filled by swimming pools, golf courses, shows, shops, and, of course, games. The casinos also appeal to the competitive instincts of a gambler. In blackjack, for instance, the player is pitted against the dealer, one to one, and the battle is usually witnessed by a gallery of his peers. In baccarat, it's the man with the shoe against the man who bets Player.

A Las Vegas psychiatrist, Irving Katz, suggests that gambling can be meaningful in a person's life because that person lacks satisfactory personal relationships. Katz says: "Many people are alienated and lonely. I find this among compulsive as well as social gamblers. They are not getting enough out of life, they are not getting contact out of life. They feel powerless. In gambling they have a sense of power. A turn of a card, the roll of the dice, the spin of a roulette wheel gives them a feeling that they are somewhat controlling their lives and luck is on their side."

Nor do you have to attend a Gamblers Anonymous meeting to learn about the damage done at the tables. No less an authority than Hank Greenspun, editor and publisher of the *Las Vegas Sun*, has written:

Public officials considering the legalization of gambling in various states should sit in the editor's chair at the Las Vegas Sun *and hear the stories of those whom gambling has harmed. This would include every legitimate merchant, owners of rental housing, and lending institutions that provide money for home purchases.*

Families have been deprived of proper food and have been unable to pay rents and mortgages because of gambling losses. Along the lines of the Surgeon General's warning on cigarette packs, those in lower income groups should be warned that gambling can become an addiction.

I have included this "downer" material in the book because nobody says you *have* to gamble. Nor does anybody say you have to lose.

There is no law limiting your thought process. You've got a mind of your own and you must put it in charge. It must grapple with temptation to discard the rules of the game as they're set out in this book. It must be clear and calm and it must constantly churn enough perspective into your thinking so that when the going is bad, you'll accept that reality and take a walk.

I said early on that gamblers were crazy. Gambling is crazy. If you can't or won't stick to a series of strict attitubes, then give up the casinos and take up crossword puzzles or cribbage.

27

The psychology of success

If by this time in the book you don't feel completely win-oriented, then it's time to ask yourself again:

Do I *really* want to win?

If the answer isn't a clear affirmative, read this slowly and carefully!

What makes a compulsive gambler?

Emotional immaturity, says a California psychologist.

Like the chronic alcoholic, the compulsive gambler is rebellious, self-centered, and ultimately self-destructive. His anti-social attitudes create feelings of guilt. His sense of guilt can be allayed only by punishment. Thus, the compulsive gambler secretly wishes to lose.

This view was expounded by Ronald A. Roston, of the University of California at Los Angeles, at an annual meeting of the American Psychological Association in Chicago.

The compulsive gambler, Roston told the meeting, "unconsciously strives to recreate and confirm infantile feelings of omnipotence by rebelling against the realities of conventional society. His rebellion, manifested in gambling, arouses guilt; by losing, he expiates guilt."

Are *you* a compulsive gambler? If you gamble more than you can comfortably afford to lose, tend to plunge when you are behind, and just can't quit when you know you should, the answer is probably *yes*.

They tell tales of a heroin addict so desperate that he will punch his own mother in the mouth to knock her teeth out so he can sell the gold in them for a fix.

I know of a banker who used to lose big and had his bank's armored car drive to Vegas with cash so he could pay off his markers. The trouble was that the money was bank money. The banker soon got his long-needed rest in the penitentiary.

A word about markers.

I've told you how to limit yourself. If you don't put rigid bars against going above your set limit and if your record of paying off is good, the casino will cheerfully help you on your way to bankruptcy. They'll stop just short of knocking out your teeth for the gold.

In the heat of play you'll sign anything to get more money. Casinos will ask you to sign a "retraction slip" saying that you are asking for more credit and want to cancel the previous limit.

Don't.

That's a simple enough instruction, yes?

Don't.

If your credit is good and your intentions are good, there is plenty of time to pay off markers.

Some of the most famous people in America are among the 3 or 4 percent who have no intention of paying off their markers. Casinos could paper their walls with them.

If the casino has tried to stretch and break you (allowed you to exceed your established limit) you can be a big sport* and pay them off, when you can. Or you

---

*Read that word as "sucker."

can settle for a partial payment.

Some casinos have collectors who are pretty persistent. They will phone you at all hours and wait on your doorstep to meet you on the way to work. They are eager because they share what they collect.

But these are not the "good old days" and nobody breaks arms and legs anymore.

I know one floorman who is decades ahead of his own bosses in his thinking. His feeling about good players who reach the point where they can't pay off the markers is that they will come to town anyway, but avoid the casinos to whom they owe money.

His philosophy is that after two years, when most unpaid markers can be considered worthless (uncollectable), he would write the markers off and mail them back to the customer with a Christmas card saying, "We appreciate your *cash* business."

No more credit, but let 'em come back to where they're known and comfortable and drop their money in friendly surroundings.

But this isn't going to be you.

28

Junkets and the comp scene

I rarely take junket flights to Las Vegas. I've already made the reasons clear. I'll repeat 'em.

I don't want to be part of a flock of sheep being led into the shearing pen.

I don't care for smoke-filled plane cabins.

I don't need anyone but me to fix my schedule: to tell me when to arrive and when to leave.

Years ago I made exceptions for the annual Sands junkets. That was pre-Hughes and the Sands was the "class" hotel, boasting a top management group led by Carl Cohen and Sandy Waterman.

During the past ten years, I've flown on only one junket plane.

Junkets are for loser-junkies. On the way home they joke about having made their "donation" or their "contribution."

I want to come and go as I please. As I explained

earlier, to insure my mobility, on most visits I rent a car.

Gone are the days when rooms were $6 a night, the New York-Vegas round trip air fare only $200 and all you can eat, and nightly mouth-watering belly-filling buffets only $1.50. Nevertheless, there are still plenty of buffets and lots of places were drinks are 50¢ a shot.

If you play for serious money, the casino will be your host. If you have a $5,000 card, your room, food and drink should be compliments of the house. And you should be entitled to pick up one coach fare. $10,000 should entitle you to bring a friend and pick up two fares. $15,000 gives you all the above plus a First Class fare. $20,000 or more should entitle you to two First Class air fare tickets (currently $1,276 from New York) and almost everything comped. Almost—because they aren't going to hand you unlimited cash—so such cash items as valet service, tips and phone calls have to be picked up by you.

(Don't forget to stop off at the cashier's window and settle your incidentals bill when you're checking out. With many hotels completely on computer, I know of one case where a medium-stakes player was told his credit was no longer good when he tried to book a junket. He had been prompt enough in paying casino markers, but he owed $6 for dry cleaning which he hadn't paid before he departed. When he received a statement from the hotel, he ignored it.)

Before I give you the casino philosophy, let me ask if you know the one about the man who was about to commit suicide by leaping into Boulder Dam.*

He was a junior bank executive and he had swindled one hundred thousand dollars from his bank—all of which he'd lost at the casino. The bank examiners were coming the next day, and when he confessed the whole thing to his wife, she packed her bags and left him.

---

*From *The World's Best Dirty Jokes* by Mr. "J."

Suddenly a voice called, "Don't jump, Sonny! There is no need to end your life! I'm a witch and I can help you!"

"I doubt it," he said sadly, "I've stolen a hundred thousand dollars from the bank, for which I'll probably be arrested tomorrow, and my wife has left me."

"Young man, witches fix anything," she said. "I'm going to perform a witch miracle." Then she said, "Alakazam! The hundred thousand dollars has been replaced and there's another hundred thousand in your safe deposit box! Alakazam! Your wife is back home again!"

He looked at her in disbelief, "Is this all true?" he asked.

"Of course," she said, "but to keep it true you must do one thing."

"Anything!" he said, "Anything!"

"You must take me to a motel and have sexual intercourse with me."

He stared at her. She was an ugly old crone, dressed in rags. Nevertheless, he agreed to her terms. He took her to a Strip motel and screwed her all night. In the morning, as he was getting dressed and combing his hair in front of the mirror, she lay on the bed watching silently. Finally, she asked, "Sonny, how old are you?"

"I'm thirty-two," he said.

"Tell me something, then," she said, "aren't you a little too old to believe in witches?"

And, indeed, dear reader, you are old enough to know there's no such a thing as something for nothing.

You pay dues, one way or another, for everything in life.

So, the casino doesn't have as its objective giving you a birthday present. Not even when it's your birthday.

You are comped and your air fare is paid only because the casino values you as a player. You are a source of profit for the business. The management assumes that if you stay at its hotel, you'll do most of your playing at its hotel. And leave most of your losses, there, too.

They're taking a chance on you but it isn't much of a gamble. They know how much your air fare comes to; that's a fixed amount. They can estimate from experience your cost to them in terms of room, food and drink bills.

I drink Tab. The next fellow wakens to champagne. The casino is willing to spring for 20% of what it expects to win from you. Thus, someone with a $20,000 card who drops all or most of it on every visit can be comped with air fare and charges of up to $4,000 without making anyone unhappy.

Few players consume the full 20%. But the unused portion helps as a cushion against those limited few who come and win and leave winners.

29

Observing your play

They're Watching You!

The "eye in the sky" consists of a series of one-way mirrors on the casino ceiling. When the money is big, there is a chance that, in addition to all the observers you can see, there may also be another pair of eyes watching from "up there."

Some casinos now have closed-circuit television. This is a sophisticated videotape system with cameras placed at strategic locations. They can zoom in on the action at any of the gaming tables as well as the counting room and the cashier cage area. Videotape is stored for later viewing when irregularities are suspected. The cameras help discourage cheating by both the players and the dealers.

I like that. I'm an honest player. I don't cheat and I don't want the casino to cheat me. That's my unspoken pact with them. Give me a fair chance at your money, and I'll give you a fair chance at mine.

It means that I don't play at little out-of-the-way

clubs which could be hurt if I won because they need the money. It means the box men will see that no shaved dice come into the game. It means the blackjack pit boss will see that nobody deals seconds. I play only where I can take some money and still leave them smiling.

They don't always smile everywhere.

For example, many of my early forays among the list of ten took place at the Riviera. It became my new Aladdin. I couldn't lose there.

Occasionally I would suffer temporary losses. I'd sign markers and they were sure they had me. But before leaving town I'd somehow win it all back, and then some.

The Riviera has a tight-assed policy on credit and a very unhappy view of winners. It doesn't like to be diddled by the dirty digit of destiny. Thus it was that on one visit (when I was staying at Caesars Palace) I played at the Riviera and on the first day won some money. Went back a few hours later and won some more.

On the second day of my visit, I walked into the Riviera. It would be at least another ten minutes before the baccarat shoe would run out and the cards shuffled. I wanted to play a full shoe so to pass the time, I walked to the dice table and called for $3,000.

My card at the Riviera was for $20,000.

I didn't owe them a dime. In past years I usually paid what I owed within two weeks after returning to New York. My word is better than gold because the value of gold fluctuates.

The shift manager hustled over to me.

"Lyle," he said, "I received word that you'll have to play for cash."

"What are you talking about?"

He was obviously uncomfortable. "I have orders. You know you took more than $25,000 cash from us yesterday, and the boys feel you should bring at least $10,000 of it back before you go on the card."

"I've got cash in a box at the Palace. You'll get anything I owe you before I leave town. And you know if I tell you that, then it's so."

"I know. I know," he said mournfully, "but I have orders. They insist that you come back with some of the cash."

"Who is 'they'?"

"Upstairs."

"Whoever is upstairs making decisions like this probably couldn't qualify as third assistant cocksucker at a Mongolian cluster-fuck."

"Lyle, I only work here. I take orders."

I walked. This so infuriated "upstairs" that later I was told I could play at the Riviera *only* for cash.

Am I angry? Of course not. They did what they thought was good for them. I have taken at least $150,000 from them, and not once have I left them a check or had to pick up a marker.

Whatever it was that I was doing, wasn't good for them.

They could do without my play. They thought I always win. I don't, though I did lots of winning there.

"LV Loves Visitors" is a bumper sticker that you'll see often on the Strip.

Las Vegas Loves Visitors—but many casinos don't love winners. They will, on occasion, ask you to leave.

Not for doing anything wrong. Nothing shady. Nothing crooked. Nothing sharp.

Just plain winning.

A cardinal sin. And one worthy of excommunication. Exclusion.

Remember now, I'm not talking about blackjack counters. That question is in the courts and will eventually be decided one way or the other.

I'm talking about honest, albeit lucky players. I'm talking about winners.

This question too eventually will have to be decided by the courts. Do you have an absolute right of access to casino tables?

I would think so, provided you put your money up and conduct yourself in an orderly manner.

Most casinos will let you strike it rich and know that eventually they'll recoup their money. You'll overstay your luck. You'll lose it back.

If you travel to another casino and lose it there, they'll console themselves with the hope that some day you'll win some there and bring it back here.

If you are going to do high stakes gambling you should confine it to resorts which are large and successful. Keep away from out-of-the-way casinos. Keep away from grind joints.

The Flamingo Capri, for example, is a sleeping giant. It will earn a mint of money. It's on the Strip but it isn't for you. It's a grind joint.

Ditto a place like the Holiday Casino. It stands in front of the Holiday Inn and so people assume they're one and the same, and good old apple pie Holiday Inn is certainly a respectable place in which to play. They're connected but only physically. The motel has nothing to do with the casino.

Now let me tell you something that I should have stressed earlier.

Your job is to win and run, right?

The casino's job is to keep you playing. The longer you play the better their chances.

It's something called DECISIONS.

DECISIONS. DECISIONS. DECISIONS.

The house wants as many decisions as possible. For example, if the percentage on a game is 2, they need fifty decisions (in theory) to take 100% of your stake.

Hilton baccarat dealers will deal so fast that you won't have a moment to scratch your head.

Decisions!

You'll find the drive to decisions everywhere. Blackjack. Roulette. Craps. Baccarat.

Dice stickmen act as carnival barkers, touting the proposition bets. You will become very conscious of the fact that you are at a table where the goal is *decisions*.

When the action is too decision-prone—too fast for you—walk away.

Look down at your ankles. There are no strings attached: no chains that bind you to stay at any table or in any casino one minute longer than you feel you want to be there.

It's worth remembering.

30

The day I did myself wrong

The incident at the Riviera happened on my *eleventh* trip.*

I haven't told you about that one, have I?

You thought I always win? Not so.

I have always won when I followed the rules and philosophy laid out in this book. I came a cropper when I allowed my discipline to erode.

The eleventh trip. I was tired. (Red light!) I was upset about something in my life having nothing to do with gambling. (Red light!)

Two red STOP signals, right?

I flew to Las Vegas from Los Angeles. I planned to spend just one day in town. I decided to go directly to a hotel midway on the Strip. Instead, I stopped off at the first place en route, the Tropicana, and played dice and blackjack until I quickly dropped almost $7,000.

---

*It was probably a bad move on their part for they might have won back a big chunk of what I lost.

171

In the parking lot I sat in my car and made my report into my trusty little Norelco. I cautioned myself.

Let me give you the first part of the report, word for word from the now "historic" tape of my first disaster in 1977—and one in which I broke every rule in my own rulebook. Here it is without a word edited:

"Well, this is the beginning of trip eleven. It's about thirteen minutes after five [A.M.] and I'm standing in front of the Beverly Hills Hotel waiting for a taxi to take me to an early Western Airlines flight to Las Vegas.

"I just counted my money and I have $21,805.65 in my pockets, and although I'm probably tired because I didn't get a helluva lot of sleep—I was exahusted after the ABA [American Booksellers Association] convention and handling the kids [2] and the dog [1] and all the garbage of sneaking the dog into the hotel* and so forth, I feel pretty good, almost elated, and I'm going to try to make this my eleventh winning trip.

"What I plan to do is go right to the Aladdin, play some dice, and maybe some baccarat and then scout around town going to a few places to win a little at each place if I can—until Bob K. arrives, which should be around 12:30, 12:35, and then spend some time showing him around. And that's the way it looks from here, and that's all there is on this pre-Las Vegas report. Next report, I suppose, after some gaming."

(*2nd Report*) "Well, I stopped off at the Tropicana and so far I'm a little too tired to do myself any good. I dropped about sixty-seven or sixty-eight hundred dollars—mostly at dice where I never got started, and

---

*Although we occupied a bungalow, the Beverly Hills Hotel no longer permits dogs even in the bungalows, so we had to smuggle Cinnamon, our six-month-old apricot poodle puppy, into the place and then tip maids and bellmen like crazy to keep them happy and quiet about the whole thing. In addition, my lady friend's seven-year-old daughter and her fourteen-year-old baby sitter were with us.

twenty-three hundred of the sixty-eight, I dropped at blackjack and now I'm on the way and I think I'll go to the Riviera and win some money at baccarat. Next report soon."

(*3rd Report*) "Man proposes but sometimes circumstance disposes! I went to the Riviera, was warmly greeted at the dice table, called for $3,000, made a few bad rolls while I was trying to push my luck, at which point I was told that the little tab on my card saying I must play for cash was still on my card. At which point I cashed in—at that point I think I'd lost about $2,600—and thanked them very much and drove over to Caesars Palace, where, at my request, they made a new shoe. And, although I started out slowly, I soon got into it and I really wasn't pressing very much. I had (mentally) committed myself to play for two full shoes (only) and I could have quit earlier and maybe walked away with more money. But they were very interesting shoes, both of them—both a little bit freaky in that in one case the bank—somebody had eleven passes on the Bank and I was on nine of those—but not with a lot of money—then toward the end I kind of gave back quite a bit because the score was then 40 Bank and 29 Player and I was convinced Player would even it out but it didn't—Bank ended up with 44 and I lost 4 substantial bets.*

"By the way, I made a few bets for the dealers including one $200 two-way [divided between dealers and starters] bet and one $100 two-way bet and won for them—so they got $600 and then I made a couple that lost so that was $800 in tips. I cashed in $16,000 and I'm going to take a count to know where I am just at this moment. (Pause.) And the count is right down to the penny, I'm ahead $7,150—though I have not left

---

*Someone who read this book in manuscript suggested I take some of this out because it contradicts some of my rigid rules. I explained that I wanted this to be a completely honest and authentic report—even to reflecting my own weaknesses.

town yet! Incidentally, regarding the two cards. On one
shoe I played on 69 hands, but only won 30. On the
second shoe I participated in 71 hands and won 32—
again winning fewer than I lost. But obviously I walked
away with a lot of money. And that's all there is for
now. I've checked into the room. I'm gonna relax, get a
haircut, take a shower now—and more later. Probably
will play some dice on the way over to Tony Pepe but
that's the way it is."

(*4th Report*) "Okay. I went down to the Aladdin
and played some dice and wasn't doing too well and, as
a matter of fact I signed markers for $9,000 in disgust
and then I made a comeback and cashed in and I was
$640 ahead. I don't even know what that brings the to-
tal to but that's where it is now."

(*5th Report*) "I went downstaris with Bob K. to
demonstrate some of the way I play baccarat. I played
one shoe. It had begun already but someone was nice
enough to let me see what had happened up to that
point. And for a while I was doing pretty good—I was
ahead five or six thousand—and then I decided to lock
it up at $3,000. I made a $3,000 show-off bet and lost
so I ended up owing $75 commission which the supervi-
sor graciously waived, and I ended up even at that
game.

"I went over to dice and there was spotty playing but
there was one guy who had an awfully good shoot—I
never did get the dice—won another $4,400. Next re-
port soon."

Now for some editorial comment. You're an expert
now so you should spot many things wrong with what
I've been doing. I arrived tired. When I got control of
myself and turned an abrasive loss into a win, I nevertheless was irritated by the Riviera action. More important—I was wandering. No goals. No limits. No departure time. No program—no planning and, therefore, *no
way to remain a winner!*

Worse, I was entertaining. I was playing games to show someone how I play. For example, had I been alone and ahead $6,000 or $7,000 at baccarat and then watched the winnings shrink and decided to lock it up, I would have locked it up. Down to $3,000 ahead and not a penny more! No question about it. But with someone at my side who was obviously impressed by the size of my bets, I couldn't resist wanting to show him how easily I could win another $3,000 in a single bet. Except that I lost.

Discipline was eroding.

The next report was the disaster warning. It started this way: "Okay, bad report. At any rate, after screwing around and showing Bob some of the town, I then did a number of things that you're never supposed to do. I bet $300 on a blackjack table because I wanted to give him [Bob] money to cover his tips and incidentals. Lost that bet and another $600 bet. And then in the course of it all, he said to me, 'Listen, are you gonna play some baccarat?' 'Cause I'd like my daughter to watch how you play. She doesn't believe you bet $4,000 on a card.' And so I put on a baccarat show and I had two incredibly bad shoes from my point of view. Quite, quite unbelievable. Like on one of them Player came up 55 times instead of the usual 34, and I was so desperate that every time the shoe came to me* I lost $4,000. I tapped out my $20,000 credit and then went into my cash. On those two shoes I lost another $32,000 cash."

I don't like the sight of blood so I won't publish the balance of the tape except to say that the total visit was a bad one.

*The person holding the shoe is called "the banker." If he makes a pass (wins the hand) he retains the shoe. When he loses a hand, the shoe goes to the next player on his right. Thus, each person at the table is given the chance to handle the shoe. As spelled out before, you can be the banker even while betting Player. You may pass the shoe at any time.

Back in New York I did some thoughtful evaluation. I knew how to win. I'd certainly proven that. Ten times in a row. Why then on my eleventh trip had I seemed to be working to lose?

Las Vegas is full of zombies and on that trip, tired beyond my own realization, I had become one of them. What happens when you're tired is that you tend to make larger bets just to wake yourself up—to stimulate yourself. I had squandered cash. I had cashed checks. I had raised my credit limits.

I knew, too, that the second worst move is to entertain someone at the gaming tables and the very worst move is to try to win some money for them.

Lady Luck has a peculiar sense of humor. Again and again I've known situations where somebody was trying to win money just to round out an amount. For example, at $19,300 a winner wants to go for $20,000. He loses it all back trying.

I know a blackjack player who, having won $5,000, decided he wanted to tip the dealer $25—but not out of his own money. So he lost it all back trying to win that $25.

The fateful words "I'd like my daughter to watch how you play" were the beginnings of a bad day at Loser's Lane.

$81,000 worth.

31

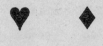

I take a new look

I was still ahead a net balance of $75,505 for eleven visits. This was consoling, but not completely.

I had gotten to be a smart ass. I had come to believe that I had beaten the system.

Obviously, I hadn't.

I surveyed what I had done. I listened to those Norelco tapes again. I analyzed my wisdoms and my stupidities.

I then developed a little 3 x 5 card which you see on the next page. It's a reflection and discipline exercise. It requires me to fill in the time, place and amount I am willing to risk, backup risk reserve and then a place to indicate to myself if I am tired, a little tired, or not tired at all.

Note the warning: DO NOT PLAY WHEN TIRED.

Since then I have returned to Las Vegas a number of times. When I used the cards I won. When I didn't, I lost.

It's as simple as that for me.

Time: _____   Place: _____

Tired? __not at all __little __zombie

  DO NOT PLAY if Zombie

Energy: __high __good __poor

  DO NOT PLAY IF POOR

Will risk: $_____

Backup $: $_____

  Outcome:

32

Return to battle

After the eleventh trip I was still a winner on balance, but much annoyed with myself. More, the experience had shaken my confidence.

Like a man who has fallen off a horse and knows he must get right back on a horse if he is ever to ride again, I headed West.

Two weeks had passed. I was alert and recharged again.

I stayed in town two days and left winning $37,740 for the visit.

I was on my way again.

When you've been lucky, you've been lucky.

Recently, I was visiting with Mitzi Briggs and her son Carl. She's the owner of the Tropicana.

I don't play often at the Trop because I know it's having a hard time (though things are getting better) and I recognize that I have some psychological resistance to taking a lot of money from the place.

This time Mitzi Briggs went to make a telephone call and to pass the time, Carl and I stood at the craps table and I played some dice. I won. No matter what I did, I won.

I was playing with comparatively small money.

It grew.

"Mother's going to be upset," Carl remarked with a smile.

We walked to the baccarat table.

I couldn't seem to lose a bet. The money grew.

"I'd better quit," I said. "I can't lose."

"Mother is going to be very upset," Carl repeated. Then: "Why don't you bet on tie?"

I made a bet on tie. It came up.

I repeated the wager. It came up again.

I was now $6,000 ahead.

"Mother's going to be *very* upset," Carl said.

"I don't know," I said. "I've done everything you suggested."

"Make a big bet on Player," Carl suggested. "Give them back a little."

I bet $2,000 on Player.

It won.

"Mother's going to be *very* upset," Carl said. I agreed and stopped playing. I was $8,000 ahead.

Mitzi Briggs wasn't all that upset although I pointed out that her phone call cost the casino $8,000. But at least I was able to show her again why I felt I shouldn't play at the Tropicana until it really flourishes.

When you've been lucky, you've been lucky.

The tie bet at baccarat brings up a peculiar thing that has happened to me.

I tell it to you because I want to tell you everything. But I tell it to you with the warning that there is no logical reason for it. None at all.

To date it is the only casino wager that has come up consistently with a percentage in favor of me.

The tie bet at baccarat pays 8 to 1. The house has a big percentage going against you.

Nevertheless, I kept feeling that ties repeat after ties more frequently than they should. There was no logical reason for this any more than there is for the belief that a shooter sevens out after his dice hit someone's hands.

I decided to check on it by keeping records. Then I decided to bet. I bet a tie after a tie.

One hundred dollars.

On my 95 full shoes a tie came up once some 605 times. It repeated 82 times. After the repeat, I take the bet down for although ties sometimes do come in sequences of 3 and 4, my records show that it's a bad bet to continue betting after the first repeat.

Investment: $60,500 at $100 on a tie wager after the first tie appeared.

Takeout: $73,800 at $900 taken down on 82 ties that repeated.

Profit: $13,300.

I tell you again that there is no reason why this wager should work. But it has worked consistently for me and I thought I'd share it with you.

33

The summing up

Keep in mind that all gambling is taking a chance. Most things in life are matters of chance and circumstance—including whether lightning will strike you before tomorrow's sun rises in the east. Your winning must be measured against the consequences of possible loss. You *can* win. Whether you win or not will depend more on what you do than what cards and dice do.

You have the ingredients in this book that can change your play and alter the outcome.

Your first challenge is yourself. Control yourself and you're a giant step forward to beating the casino.

It's possible, but *only you* can make it probable!
Luck to you!

Your Guide to Casino Winning

THE NINE COMMANDMENTS

1. Never gamble when you are tired or unhappy.

2. Never gamble for more money than you can comfortably afford to lose.

3. Never forget that the longer you stay at any casino table, the larger are the odds that you will walk away a loser.

4. Never begin to play unless you know at exactly what loss point and/or win point you will quit.

5. Always place at least ¾ of your winnings in a casino or hotel-provided safe deposit box. Refuse to gamble further if you lose the other 25%.

6. If you feel "negative" stop. Do other things until your mood changes. Depressed gamblers rarely win. And the tables are always there for when your attitudes/hunches change.

7. Avoid playing when you feel insecure or lonely or don't have a clear sense of discipline about a plan of action and a schedule of goals.

8. When on a losing streak, don't try to recoup by increasing the size of your wagers. On the contrary, cut them. Increase wagers when on a win

streak. In other words, limit your losses but let
your winnings run.

9. Always keep in mind that the real struggle isn't
    between you and the casino. It's between you
    and yourself.